I0062256

HOW TO WIN

THE BUSINESS WAR

HOW TO WIN

THE BUSINESS WAR

Written by

Richard Knight

Edited by: AnnMarie Reynolds

Published by: begin-a-book Independent Publishers

www.beginabook.com/info@beginabook.com

begin-a-book

First Published in Great Britain in 2025
by begin-a-book Independent Publishers (www.beginabook.com)

Copyright © Richard Knight 2025

All rights reserved. No part of this publication may be reproduced, stored in or introduced into a retrieval system, or transmitted, in any form, or by any means (electronic, mechanical, photocopying, recording or otherwise) without the prior written permission of the Publisher or the Author.

The right of Richard Knight to be identified as the author of this work has been asserted by him in accordance with the Copyright, Designs and Patents Act 1988.

This book is sold subject to the condition that it shall not, by way of trade or otherwise, be lent, resold, hired out, or otherwise circulated without the publisher's prior consent in any form of binding or cover other than that in which it is published and without a similar condition including this condition being imposed on the subsequent purchaser.

ISBN (paperback): 978-1-915353-41-2
ISBN (digital ebook): 978-1-915353-42-9

Cover design (front) by Tim Burdett, TBB Design. (www.tbbdesign.co.uk)
With extensive experience as a graphic designer, Tim Burdett brings a deep passion for creative design and a strong track record across a diverse range of projects. At TBB Design, he continues to deliver thoughtful, high-quality solutions that reflect his commitment to excellence and love for the craft.

To all small business owners.

May your success continue to grow and empower the world around you.

CONTENTS

Acknowledgements   10

Introduction   13

Sample/Bonus Article   15

SECTION ONE - BUSINESS AND COACHING   17

  1. I Don't Need A Coach Or Mentor   18
  2. Do As I Say Or Do As I Do?   20
  3. Do Or Do Not ~ There Is No Try   22
  4. Do You Follow Up?   24
  5. Do You Prepare For The What Ifs?   26
  6. Do You Think For Yourself?   28
  7. Do Your Fears Limit You?   30
  8. How Much Time Do You Spend On Planning?   32
  9. Goal Setting ~ Why It Is Vital To Success   34
  10. How Do You Eat An Elephant?   36
  11. How Good Are Our Communication Skills?   38
  12. If You Don't Look For It You Won't Find It   41
  13. Just How Important Is Respect?   42
  14. Readers Are Leaders   44
  15. Simple Acts Of Kindness ~ How They Help Us All 46
  16. The Battle Scars Of Business Ownership   48
  17. Life Is Built On Thin Threads   50
  18. What Can We Learn From Gareth Southgate?   52
  19. What Did I Learn? ~ My First Two Years In Business 54
  20. Wheel Of Life   56

SECTION TWO - ME & MY BUSINESS, YOU & YOUR BUSINESS   59

  21. Where Did It All Start? ~ Personal Development 60
  22. Are We Really All In The Same Boat?   62
  23. Be The Hero Of Your Own Story   64
  24. Are You Stuck In The Maze?   66
  25. Do You Have A Single-Minded Attitude To Life? 68
  26. Embrace Life's Experiences ~ They Shape Us   70
  27. Have You Ever Said, 'It's Not Fair!'?   72
  28. Just Working Hard ~ Is It Enough?   74

29.	Taking Responsibility In Everything You Do	76
30.	Theory or Experience?	78
31.	We Have To Live With The Choices We Make	80
32.	What Is Your Why?	82
33.	What Makes Us Who We Are?	84
34.	What Makes Us Stand Out From The Crowd?	86
35.	You Are The Problem To Your Problems	88
36.	You Are What You Do ~ Action!	90

SECTION THREE - (BUSINESS) SELF-DEVELOPMENT   **93**

37.	Beware Of Idiots Wrapped In Tin Foil	94
38.	Stop Pulling Yourself In All Directions	96
39.	Do You Ask Why?	98
40.	Discipline ~ Goal Setting vs Goal Achieving	100
41.	Are You A Conformist?	102
42.	Don't Be Frightened To Ask For Help	104
43.	You Need To Get Out Of Your Comfort Zone	106
44.	Big Boy/Girl Pants Time!	108
45.	Do You Create Successful Habits?	110
46.	Do You Feel Like You Are Going 'Up' The 'Down' Elevator?	112
47.	Do You Make Excuses?	114
48.	How Do Negative Situations Affect Your Attitude?	116
49.	How Do You Cope With Setbacks?	118
50.	How Good Are You At Adapting?	120
51.	How Strong Are Your Commitments?	122
52.	Optimist Or Pessimist?	124
53.	Trust	126
54.	What Do We Say When We Talk To Ourselves?	128
55.	You Are Not Going To Get Out Of Life Alive	130
56.	Are You Born To Stand Out Or Just Fit In?	132

SECTION FOUR - RUNNING A SUCCESSFUL BUSINESS   **135**

57.	Begin With The End In Mind	136
58.	Choices ~ How Important Are They?	138
59.	Business Is Not A Template	140
60.	Business Today Is Different ~ We Must Learn From The Past	142
61.	Do You Let Your Circumstances Define You?	144
62.	Do You Think You Are Lucky?	146
63.	Do You See Suppliers As Part Of Your Team?	148

64. People Buy From People 150

65. Reliability - Can Everyone Rely On You To Deliver? 152

66. Rest If You Must, But Don't Quit 154

67. So, How Do You Run A Successful Business? 156

68. Technology Is An Addition, Not A Replacement 158

69. Under Promise, Over Deliver 160

70. What Have We Learned From Situations Outside Our Control? .. 162

71. Are You Top Of Mind? 164

SECTION FIVE - GROWING YOUR BUSINESS   **167**

72. Networking - Why Is It Important To A Small Business? ... 168

73. Are You Building A Win-Win Business? 170

74. Are You Future Proofing Your Income? 172

75. Building A Successful Business ~ Where Does It Start? 174

76. Do You Know Your Target Market? 176

77. Does Your Business Appear To Be Going Backwards? 178

78. Negative Or Positive Mindset? 180

79. Stuff Doesn't Just Happen 182

80. What Are You Frightened Of? 184

81. Adversity ~ What Can We Learn? 186

SECTION SIX - BEING BUSINESS SAVVY   **189**

82. Don't Buy Things You Can't Afford 190

83. Don't Build Your Castle In Someone Else's Garden 192

84. Do You Really Understand Networking? 194

85. How Good Are You At Due Diligence? 196

86. How Good Are You At Spotting Opportunities? 198

87. How Networking Can Save (& Make) You Thousands Of Pounds .. 200

88. The Power Of Effective Communication 202

89. Why, Only When It Really Hurts, Do So Many Take Action? .. 204

90. Change ~ Are Our Businesses Set Up To Cope? 206

SECTION SEVEN - YOUR BUSINESS AND THE FUTURE   **209**

91. How Are You Building For The Future? 210

92. How Will Your Next Chapter Read? 212

93. It's Time For A Paradigm Shift 214

94. Should I Quit? 216

95. Tough Times Don't Last; Tough People Do 218

SECTION EIGHT - BUSINESS AND MONEY   221

   96. Cost Or Investment?   222

   97. Do You Know Your Numbers?   224

   98. How Future-Proof Is Your Income?   226

   99. Put Money Away For A Rainy Day   228

   100. Two Sides To Every Story ~ Straight From The Heart 230

ACKNOWLEDGEMENTS

Where do I start on this one?

Since 1982 when I first started my business journey, so many people have had a massive impact on my life and I don't want to miss anyone out - which I know I will if I start mentioning them by name!

Those I have met along the way will know who they are and, if you are reading this book and I know you personally, then without a doubt, in some way - large or small - you will have had a positive affect on my life and possibly some of the decisions I have made.

One person I do want to mention by name and dedicate this book to, is my beautiful wife, Denise. Denise has been my rock since we married in 1981, always by my side cheering me on and standing by my decisions - the good and the bad! Along with our two beautiful daughters, Lauren and Gemma, I have kept you at the heart of every choice I made because my mission was to build a lifestyle for the two of us and a legacy for Lauren and Gemma. Not a lavish lifestyle or legacy, and not just a financial one either, simply a happy and comfortable existence which, with your continuing support, I believe I have done.

I am, as I said, concerned I will miss some important people out, so I thought I'd include sections/chapters of my life in the hope that if I haven't mentioned you by name, you'll recognise yourself in one of these:

Network Marketing - thanks to all those who started me on my journey and are still with me today. Meeting you and the help you've given have been a massive part of my life. Thank you.

Business Networking - I have met so many great people at networking meetings. Many have become outsourced suppliers whom I have trusted to look after aspects of my business. With your support I was able to focus on the parts of my business I was good at, and leave the rest to you!

My Business Team - where would I have been without my employees? I didn't get it right all the time, and for those of you who were with me during the 2008/2009 recession, I thank you from the bottom of my heart. I would not have got through those times without you. We pulled through as a team and came out stronger. Thank you.

Family and Friends - my family (close friends are also family) who have kept me sane - and still keep me sane - thank you. We laugh a lot, we cry a bit, we get very emotional at times. We are there for each other. We have fun in each other's company and we very much support each other. Those fun times we share are so important because, without these, nothing else would have been possible. So I thank you deeply.

Finally, I want to thank AnnMarie who, without her help, this book would not have come into being. It started as a number of articles that I had written during 2020 and 2021 and posted on LinkedIn. AnnMarie (from *begin-a-book Writing Services and Independent Publishers*), has been instrumental in putting these together in format that is easy to use and will offer practical help and support to everyone reading this book. Thank you, AnnMarie, for your dedication.

INTRODUCTION

Richard Knight
Pictured with his wife, Denise.

My business journey began in 1982 when I was 24 years old. Through a friend I was introduced to the concept of Network Marketing and before long, I was hooked. Attending networking meetings and surrounding myself with successful and success-minded people taught me so much, including the 'right' way to do business. Any tips and tricks they shared I eagerly consumed, filing them away for the time when I would become a business owner myself.

Further, their positivity and 'go-getter' attitudes were infectious - and I wanted more! Listening to motivational and inspirational cassette tapes and CDs (it was the 80s!) provided me with that 'something extra' and I would listen to the words of national and international business titans for many an hour. Still this wasn't enough; I wanted to learn everything I could so that when the time was right for me to become a business owner myself, I would be as prepared as I could. The next step, then, was personal development books which I devoured alongside the tapes and CDs and networking meetings. The combination of all three activities soon paid off and the impact on my life was so incredibly positive that by 1987, I was ready to set up my own advertising agency.

That's not to say everything was rosy - far from it - but the time I had taken to learn as much as I could before jumping in with both feet, meant I was equipped to face those inevitable challenges. I went on to run my business for over 33 years before selling it as a successful going concern in August 2020. Alongside that I built a substantial property portfolio meaning I can now enjoy a comfortable retirement on my own terms.

If that all sounds too good to be true, I'm here to tell you it's not. Business networking holds the key, it really does, but the problem is that too many small and medium sized business owners overlook it.

At the start of 2020, I made a commitment to write one business article every week for two years. My goal was to pass on my passion for business networking, and to help and encourage every small and medium business owner that I could reach to look at their business differently. To start working ON their businesses and not remain firmly stuck IN their businesses - because that is the only way to build and maintain a successful company.

Once I had completed my article-writing mission, I reflected on their true value and realised that the best way to help as many business owners as I could, was to combine them in an easy to read book format.

In the following pages you will find articles packed full of universal advice which can be applied to any business regardless of type, size or business model. And the best bit?

This advice is tried and tested!

I've balanced the successes against the mistakes and provided simple exercises along the way. Everything is presented in an easy to follow format which will allow you to instantly identify the areas most relevant to you and your business. You don't need to read the book cover to cover - in fact, I would actively discourage this. To make the most of this book I strongly recommend you check out the contents list at the beginning of each section and then flip to the most relevant page.

Keep this book on your desk or nearby you as you work. That way, when those sticky moments arise, it will be immediately to hand.

I want you to think of *'How To Win The Business War'* as your very own *'knight in shining armour'*, ready to ride into battle at the flick of a page.

What to expect from this book:

Running a business can feel like an uphill struggle. It can be overwhelming when the ramification of each decision weighs heavy - but remember, you are your own warrior. You have everything you need within you to succeed. It's not about the number in your army, it's about the tactics you deploy.

The pages of this book will help guide your decisions, shape your business strategy and disarm the naysayers.

You CAN win the business war.

Read on to discover how!

(Facing page shows sample/bonus article)

HOW PREPARED ARE YOU?

"By failing to prepare you are preparing to fail."
~ Benjamin Franklin

I'm just going to put this out there:

We learn so much more from negative situations than we do from positive ones.

Here's why:

When things are *trucking along nicely* and we *have no challenges*, we don't learn. Everything stays the same so we continue along in our same comfortable way.

When we are *faced with adversity* we will always be in a position to learn, because we have to take action. Taking action teaches us new skills and helps us to understand more about ourselves and our businesses, although *only if the actions we take are positive.*

Great, but what does a positive action look like?

- Adding a new income stream to reduce our financial vulnerability.
- Be open to opportunities outside of our comfort zones.
- Read business books and learn from others.
- Hang out with other business owners via networking and similar events.
- Communicate with your clients and offer reassurance that you will be able to weather the storm.

If we are not presented with challenges then, arguably, we don't need to do any of these things, yet, if we haven't prepared our businesses for the unknowns by using positive actions, then we will be in a whole host of trouble when faced with adversity.

~ ~ ~ ~

1 Section One

Business and Coaching

1. I DON'T NEED A COACH OR MENTOR
2. DO AS I SAY OR DO AS I DO?
3. DO OR DO NOT - THERE IS NO TRY
4. DO YOU FOLLOW UP?
5. DO YOU PREPARE FOR THE 'WHAT IFS'?
6. DO YOU THINK FOR YOURSELF?
7. DO YOUR FEARS LIMIT YOU?
8. HOW MUCH TIME DO YOU SPEND ON PLANNING?
9. GOALSETTING - WHY IT IS VITAL TO SUCCESS
10. HOW DO YOU EAT AN ELEPHANT?
11. HOW GOOD ARE OUR COMMUNICATIONS SKILLS?
12. IF YOU DON'T LOOK FOR IT, YOU WON'T FIND IT
13. JUST HOW IMPORTANT IS RESPECT?
14. READERS ARE LEADERS
15. SIMPLE ACTS OF KINDNESS - HOW THEY HELP EVERYONE
16. THE BATTLE SCARS OF BUSINESS OWNERSHIP - SINCE 1987
17. LIFE IS BUILT ON THIN THREADS
18. WHAT CAN WE LEARN FROM GARETH SOUTHGATE?
19. WHAT DID I LEARN? - MY FIRST TWO YEARS IN BUSINESS
20. WHEEL OF LIFE

~ 1 ~

I DON'T NEED A COACH OR MENTOR

"A coach is someone who sees beyond your limits,
and guides you to greatness!" ~ Michael Jordan

I wonder how many professional athletes have said, "I don't need a coach or mentor, I can succeed on my own."?

Probably many, but none that have gone on to greatness. Why then, do so many businesses think they can achieve success without a coach, mentor or advisor to help them along the journey?

I have been in business since 1982. I started my own conventional business in 1987 and took that right through to its sale in 2016 before finally exiting in 2020. I also built other businesses during this period and the one thing they all had in common was the mentor who was by my side, guiding me, ensuring I stayed on the right track. Often, I am asked: was it worth it?

You bet your life it was, in fact, I had several mentors - all people who had proven successes in life and business. Peers who could align with my values and bring experience and support.

Yet, within the small business community, I have found a reluctance to engage a coach or mentor, and I am unsure why. I can only think that business owners believe they know it all and don't need help, or that they look at it as a cost rather than an investment.

In my opinion, anyone we outsource to **should add value** to our business. They should be working with us to help us get the best results. Their offering needs to be helping us to grow our business and not simply become a vehicle for them to line their pockets. If you find yourself outsourcing and whomever you've engaged **doesn't add value** to your business, please stop using them. But crucially, **don't stop outsourcing**!

We are all looking for our 'Knights in shining armour' and not 'imposters wrapped in tin foil', so it's a matter of realising you have yet to find your Knight and continuing the search. You will find them, I promise.

I have been networking now for over thirty years and the help and support out there is truly phenomenal, yet so many business owners will not even strike up a conversation with a coach or mentor - often because they don't think they can afford their services.

When we think that we cannot afford another's service, we begin to believe it is more cost-effective to continue on our own but I have news for you. It is definitely not more cost-effective.

Further, if a business owner is reluctant to even engage in conversation with a coach or mentor, how do they know whether the services are affordable?

The key is to stop looking at outsourcing as a cost and consider it an investment in your business. This way, you will *see* things differently and start to *do* things differently which will inevitably mean a different (and more preferable) outcome.

You need to find the right coach or mentor, though. The Knight who can use their personal business experience to demonstrate how they can support yours. When you hear someone saying that they 'understand what you are going through', that is infinitely powerful, even more so if they allow you to see that they have been there themselves.

Think also of the bigger picture. It's not just about a coach or mentor, it's about their network, too. Who else do they know? Can they put you in touch with potential customers, for example.

My personal database of contacts has been incredibly valuable to my clients, to the point I consider it FREE added value. I will facilitate introductions between professionals who I know will benefit each other, but not in an HR way.

As a coach or mentor, we can point our clients in the right direction and connect them with those who will support their journey in many different ways and, as a business, you can rely on your Knight (when you've found the right one) to provide you with the best expertise and advice they can.

They've been there before, after all and they've likely done what you're trying to do and almost certainly made more than a few mistakes, so let them help you.

The cost of hiring a coach or mentor is, without a doubt, less of a cost to your business than an avoidable and reputational damaging mistake would be.

~ ~ ~ ~

~ 2 ~

DO AS I SAY, OR DO AS I DO?

"You are what you do, not what you say you'll do."
~ C G Jung

"Do as I tell you," is a comment we have all undoubtedly heard through the years, perhaps from our parents but maybe in the workplace, too. The problem with this comment comes if we realise that the person asking us to **'do'** is not actually **'doing'** the same thing themselves. This can (and often does) lead to resentment. If, however, the person asking us to **'do' is** showing us by example, then not only is it easier for us to see the reason for their request, but we will automatically have a greater respect for them.

Fast forward a few years and we are running our own businesses or holding down a senior position within a company. It is our job to delegate, to ask others to undertake certain roles and duties, however it is much easier to achieve this if we lead by example. Why? Because talk is cheap and if you are asking your staff or colleagues to do something that you have not done yourself, how can you expect it of them?

In my opinion we need to 'walk the walk and talk the talk' or, in the words of C G Jung: "We are **what** we do, not what we **say** we'll do."

A great example came when we were faced with the COVID-19 pandemic. It was December 2021, the busiest time of year for many businesses, yet we in the UK were being asked to 'work from home'. For health reasons this made perfect sense to the majority, however when we realised that some of the very people issuing this edict were not doing the same, it created a negativity and resentment which ultimately led to many heads rolling.

A few years down the line, though, and despite the protests, many people are still 'working from home' which, in my opinion, has made us lazier. Those currently searching for new employment are often asking for a 'work from home arrangement' as part of their package - something that would have been unheard of pre-pandemic.

In my experience, working from home is lonely and can have a negative impact on our mental health and well-being. It also directly affects businesses that thrive on us 'going out' to work, such as sandwich shops, coffee shops and restaurants.

Working from home has also led to an overall apathy when it comes to leaving the safety and comfort of our lounge and onesie. Pubs, nightclubs, sporting events, theatres ... the list goes on, are still struggling to rebuild post-pandemic, simply because we have become comfortable at home. We can make our own meals. Watch our own movies. Entertain others in our front rooms. The benefits of going out to work and socialise have almost certainly been watered down by the pandemic.

Of course, COVID-19 was not the fault of those who told us to 'stay at home', however the fact that they (in some cases) did not follow the same advice, caused a disconnect between the general population and those in power. If they had chosen to '**do as I do**' and not '**do as I say**', would we be well on the way to pre-pandemic levels of activity and productivity?

It is, perhaps, a rhetorical question, though think how you felt when you were unable to see relatives, loved ones, friends, colleagues, when you missed the office banter or the general hubbub of the local cafe. Were you angry when you discovered that those in power were on occasion, doing the very thing they were asking us not to do?

My guess is that you were, and that's the thing about '**do as I say, or do as I do**'. We have a responsibility to look after our families, but we also have a responsibility to look after those upon whom our decisions impact, and then only way we can demonstrate that responsibility is by treating them with respect.

Respect is a two-way street. We cannot expect their respect and loyalty, if we are not willing to give them ours.

The impact of decisions we make on other's behalves might seem short-term when made, but in reality, most decisions leave a legacy that lasts weeks, months, years, decades even.

As a business owner or leader, make sure that the 'decision legacy' you leave behind is one of which you can be proud.

~ ~ ~ ~

DO OR DO NOT ~ THERE IS NO TRY

"No! Try not. Do, or do not. There is no try."
~ George Lucas

I love this quote and really rip into people who say, *"I will try"*. You cannot try anything. You either do it, or you don't do it. Anyone who tells me they will 'try' is often signalling their intention to 'not' do it.

How many times have you invited someone to a party and they say they will *try* to make it and you know damn well they are not going to be there?

To **try** something is to **do nothing**.

"I will try," is as weak a statement as you will ever hear - so please don't say it. Remember, we spend a large part of our day talking to ourselves and what we often forget is that this internal dialogue has power. Lots of power. What we tell ourselves has a massive impact on who and what we become, therefore, we have to be careful how we talk to ourselves. We cannot '**try**', we have to '**do**'.

To be successful in life you need to make a solid commitment and, one of the best ways to make this commitment is to verbalise your intention. If you can, verbalise this to someone you trust and who will hold you accountable because this is the key. **Be accountable.** If not to yourself, then let someone else hold that accountability for you. Making a decision to do something and then having the discipline and commitment to do it is what counts. **And you need to stick to it, no matter what.**

By focusing on the DO, you are focusing on what really matters. It really is true that we can achieve anything in life that we want, be whoever we want - the only limitations are those in our mind that we place upon ourselves. In the first article, *I DON'T NEED A COACH OR MENTOR*, I talked about different actions achieving different outcomes and it is the same here.

None of us can get from where we are to where we want to be with the same mindset that has got us to where we currently are. FACT.

Of course, I understand that changing your mindset is not easy, but a good place to start is by looking at those you are spending your time with and taking advice from. Are they people who are truly supporting you, people who lift you up and tell you that you can do it? Or are they constantly dragging you down? Even though we may not realise it, we are all products of those with whom we spend time, so it's important that we surround ourselves with people who can support rather than discourage.

Another good place to start when it comes to business mindset is to lean on a coach or mentor (see article 1), because more often than not, they are where you want to be. They've made the journey and proven their success so their influence will only be positive.

Similarly, you may find your support network in places you've not looked before - perhaps colleagues at work or a particular group of friends. When it comes to changing your mindset, to an extent it doesn't matter who is in your support network, as long as they are lifting you and up and not dragging you down.

If you are going to employ a business coach or mentor, or indeed anyone else to help you '*do*' and achieve the '*do*', then make sure to check out their references, reviews and success rates. So many of us plunge headlong into one course or another - often spending thousands - only to be hugely disappointed when the results are not as we expected.

We are the only ones who have the **power to change our outcome**, but here's the thing. The fact that we have the power, means **we absolutely can**. There is nothing stopping us. Take it from me:

You can be whoever you want to be and you can do whatever you want to do.

All you have to do is **BELIEVE IN YOURSELF**.

~ ~ ~ ~

~ 4 ~

DO YOU FOLLOW UP?

*"Diligent follow up and follow through will set you apart from
the crowd and communicate excellence."*
~ John C Maxwell

I remember listening to a business tape (yep, I'm that old!) many years ago entitled, "Follow Up Is 50% Of Your Business" - and it really is. I am constantly amazed at the number of businesses who communicate with a client or a potential new client and do not follow up. Why not? I guarantee that if you do follow up it will generate more business. If it doesn't, then you're doing something wrong.

Following up is not just about chasing the next piece of business, it's integral to the whole communication process. I have heard so many situations where business owners do a presentation or a quote after request from a potential customer - and then do not follow up. If you are guilty of this, you are in danger of creating the impression that you don't care and you expect the client to come to you. Which I am sure, is not remotely true.

Following up shows that you care and it is the next logical stage in the (business) process.

I had a situation recently where I asked a builder (who I've used before and know pretty well) for a quote. Despite visiting to discuss my needs, he never bothered to provide the actual quote. Why would he take the time to come and see me and then not even bother to contact me again? Especially when there was a good chance of securing my business considering our previous connection.

Tradespeople in general are poor at communication, but it's not just tradespeople who fall into this trap. If business owners learned how to follow up properly, it would generate them more business without a shadow of a doubt. And it would help them to build better relationships with their customers.

I think a big part of following up is about keeping in touch with a customer, showing you care about them and their business. A simple call to check all is okay goes a long way to improving business/client relationships and, taking it a step further, try asking if there is anything you can do to make things easier for them. Is there a way you can support their business? Taking a few minutes to make that call or write them an email will really impact your business in a positive way.

What, then, happens if you don't follow up or keep in touch?

At best, another business owner may come along and contact one of your customers. At worst, they will offer a similar product or service, keep in touch with your client, build a relationship with your customer and you will lose the business.

None of us have a divine right to customers. We have to constantly and consistently work on our relationships and, when times are hard, it's even more important to keep in touch.

Sometimes we might avoid reaching out for fear of a difficult conversation but please, NEVER ignore difficult conversations with a customer. Even if something has gone wrong and you are so consumed with guilt that you go quiet and ignore it - you have to overcome this fear. Ignoring an issue will never solve it. Instead, sort out the problem quickly and to the customer's satisfaction. The result will almost certainly be a relationship that is stronger than before.

Work at building strong relationships with all your customers - old and new - and keep in touch regularly. There are so many good reasons for doing this, not least of which is showing that you care. And the overall gain?

You may court a potential client for years but, when they are ready to commit, they will commit to you and might ultimately become your best customer. You never know.

One thing is guaranteed, though:

Fail to follow up and there is no way you will become their first choice - for anything.

~ ~ ~ ~

~ 5 ~

DO YOU PREPARE FOR THE 'WHAT IFS'?

"Let our advance worrying become our advance thinking and planning." ~ Winston Churchill

FAILING TO PLAN IS PLANNING TO FAIL

Having run a small business since 1987, it never ceases to amaze me how few businesses plan anything. Most of us spend more time planning a birthday party or a holiday than we spend planning our business journey.

Taking time out to plan the future of your business is vital for its continued success, but - and this is key - most of the time we are too close to the 'action' to plan effectively. We will see what we want to see or expect to see rather than what is actually there, which is why I believe all businesses (no matter their size) should source external help when it comes to business planning.

I know that, without prior preparation and planning, my business would not have survived, and it definitely wouldn't have thrived as it did for over thirty years. When I sold the business it was entirely my decision based on my long-term plan. It wasn't always easy, so don't think I am saying that it is. Tough times can be mentally draining, but without planning, you might not make it through at all.

It is natural for any business owner to be concerned about their business and/ or specific aspects of it but if you are spending all your time working IN your business, then it is critical to make some adjustments which allow you to also work ON your business. If you don't do this, your chances of continued success will be severely limited, especially if you are unable to change and adapt to outside factors.

What, for example, would you do if a key member of staff left? Or you lost your biggest client? Or there was an economic downturn and recession?

It's not unhealthy to be worried about your business' survival, but in order to give it the best chance you need to think about and plan for potential eventualities.

'What ifs' will always be there, they will always happen and they are cyclical. Often coming around every five to ten years so, if you've already been through one and not made any changes as a result - shame on you. You should never fail with the same excuse twice.

We cannot claim that our businesses failed due to external situations. Yes, the external situation (economy for example) may have exacerbated the problem, but the failure of our company is more likely due to us **failing to plan** for that situation.

During the 2008 recession (more like a depression as far as I was concerned!), the media made it seem far worse than it ever should have been. As a result a lot of good businesses were forced to close. Mine scraped through but only because I had put plans in place five or six years previously. It took a further five years to totally recover from the 2008 recession and I know that without this planning, my business would not have made it.

In recent times I've known of three local businesses that have been forced to close. One had an 87-year history, another a 126-year history and the final, a 200 year-history. Every single one blamed external circumstances for their demise but closer inspection revealed a complete lack of planning. These were family businesses that had continued to run in the same way for the duration, generation after generation with little to no thought given to the future. Bad decision.

It's true that generations ago, businesses underwent less change than they do today which is due in no small part to improvements in modern technology. Some practices and methods that have 'always worked' may be outdated and unlikely to work now in what is a very different business landscape. It's the same as I've mentioned in previous articles - if we keep doing the same thing then our business will keep going in the same direction. And we can pretty much guarantee that direction will not be forwards.

With all the challenges we face as a world, it is imperative now more than ever to plan so don't be afraid to ask for outside help, though check their credentials. Remember: *"If you don't check credentials you will end up with an imposter wrapped in tinfoil and not your Knight in shining armour."* Instead, follow the wise words of Winston Churchill and you won't go wrong.

~ ~ ~ ~

~ 6 ~

DO YOU THINK FOR YOURSELF?

"Think for yourself or others will think for you - without think-
ing of you." ~ Henry David Thoreau

Running your own business requires a totally different level of thinking. When you work for someone else, other people are generally making decisions for you but when you run your own business, it's all on you.

I often find that those who have been employed for the majority of their lives, appear to have difficulty making decisions of thinking of themselves. This, though can be motivated by a fear of repercussion. Perhaps they did think for themselves once and it went badly.

When you become a small business owner you have to shift from employee to employer mentality fast, and this is not helped by the fact that there is a massive difference between the two levels of thinking. It does take time to transition to a business owner mindset, but you need to expedite that process if you can. Otherwise the success of your (fledgling) business will be negatively impacted.

My expectations, when I meet business owners for the first time is to hear unique ideas and a diversity of thinking, yet there are so many who have been unable to shift between employee and employer mentality, thus remaining content for others to make any important decisions. This is not ideal. Especially if those you are relying on to make decisions have no direct connection to your business. If they do not have any connection to your business then arguably they have no right to dictate what should be done - and a good way to sense-check this is by remembering the following:

Your business success directly impacts your income as well
as the health and well-being of your family.

As the opening quote says: "If you **don't think for yourself**, others will think *for you without thinking of you.*"

In short, these people do not care about the impact on you, your business or your family, so why listen to them?

If you allow someone else to do your thinking, they will totally control you so remember this:

> That person does not put food on your table or look after
> your family. That is your responsibility.

As business owners and leaders it is critical that we do our own thinking, for right or for wrong, and the best way to do that is to think about ourselves. Not in a selfish way, but in the ways our decisions will affect those around us.

Think about the impact any decisions you make will have on your family and therefore make decisions that affect us and our loved ones rather than those who have little care for our well-being.

Don't blindly follow guidelines regardless of where these are from. It's important to ask questions and make sure that every decision you make is - to the best of your knowledge - right for you and your business.

~ ~ ~ ~

DO YOUR FEARS LIMIT YOU?

"If you can't face your fears, they limit you."
~ Robin Sharma (adapted)

We are all fearful of something, however we can only move on once we overcome those fears. No matter what they are.

FEAR = False Expectations Appearing Real

In life, we love being in our comfort zone because there is no challenge or fear in that zone. The problem is, if we stay in our comfort zone, we won't progress and that's when we can find fear really holding us back.

Fears can be anything from a fear of spiders to changing jobs, and facing these for the first time is incredibly uncomfortable. Over time though, we will become more comfortable and will often wonder why we felt so fearful in the first place.

Fear limits us, yet, according to Alan Cohen (author), *"Limits exist only in our minds."*

Think about that for a second. Do your limits exist in reality?

We need to be challenged. The human race thrives on challenges and on overcoming these, which is not always easy. When we do overcome them, though, that's when we grow.

We are born without fear nor baggage. Fears are weights we collect as we go through life, often influenced by our parents and those around us. As business owners we have already stepped outside our comfort zone. We do not have the certainty of a job or regular income and will encounter all manner of fears. Facing these is what allows us to build our business - but we are often guilty of pushing these things to the bottom of the list, doing those with which we are comfortable first. Yet, the most gains are always found in these areas. The ones we fear.

It can be helpful to get into the habit of addressing those issues which give you the most discomfort, first. It's not easy, but the sense of achievement and accomplishment is huge.

If you struggle to face these challenges on your own, talk to someone who has been where you are. Let them guide you, advise you and hold your hand.

When we are put under pressure, our ability to rationalise is negatively affected which in turn, increases our fear. Things which may have seemed small before, multiply in size once the pressure on our shoulders increases. That's when we are unable to think clearly.

If you find yourself in this situation then as well as reaching out for support, it's also helpful to consider ways of shifting or pivoting your business to reduce some of the pressure. So many small business owners have had to shift direction (especially since the pandemic) to ensure they remain solvent.

Changing focus is not a sign of failure.

Far from it. It is an indication of your strength as a business owner. You have recognised the limitations (you have potentially placed on yourself) and are challenging them. Fear does not need to be prohibitive.

Fear can in fact, be freeing.

Many business owners are more than happy to offer advice and support - often without cost - so try reaching out. You never know what fears they will help you become free from.

~ ~ ~ ~

~ 8 ~

HOW MUCH TIME DO YOU SPEND ON PLANNING?

"Failing to plan is planning to fail." ~ Alan Lakein

As I sit writing this article in September of 2020, I am looking forward to going to watch a live Rugby game this afternoon - the first since the start of the global pandemic. There have, however, been a few issues with season ticket holders being able to gain access to their tickets which led me to reflect on the importance of planning.

Over the last 33 years since I set up my advertising Agency, I have been surprised at the lack of planning implemented by many businesses. Some plan literally nothing and simply wait for the s**t to hit the fan. Planning, when it came to accessing our Rugby tickets, was definitely not high on their agenda.

Live sport virtually ended (in the UK) around the middle of March 2020. Though we were uncertain when, it was a given that at some point in the future, we would see its return. What was also fairly obvious was that the number of spectators would initially be drastically reduced to allow for compliance with safety measures around the pandemic.

My view, taking all of these things into account, was that the time between sport ending and re-commencing (in this instance, 24 weeks), could be taken for planning the next stage when the turnstiles would once again be open. I was therefore delighted when my club was one of the first to allow spectators back into the ground. Until we hit a problem.

The club made a decision to allow 3,000 spectators (season ticket holders) into the game. This number represented a fifth of the ground capacity at 15,000, so a method of selection for the lucky ticket recipients was outlined in an email to all season ticket holders. We would need to enter a ballot which would be drawn a few days prior to the game. If we were successful, we would then be allocated a ticket to purchase in time for the big day.

I was one of the lucky ones. Through the ballot I was awarded a ticket for a match that was four days away. We were instructed that in order to attend, we must purchase our tickets before 5pm on the day before the game. Fantastic. So far so good. As match day drew near, though, I noticed rumblings on social media from many ticket holders who were unable to 'see' their ticket in the basket and thus could not purchase them. I, sadly, was one of those affected so I began sending emails to the club, only to be told that my ticket was there, in my basket, waiting for me to checkout. It most definitely wasn't.

I had to write two further emails and provide screen shots to prove that my tickets were not in my basket before the issue was finally resolved. I purchased it and printed it out just in time to attend.

At the match I did a rough head count and reckoned there were probably about 1,800 supporters there out of a possible 3,000. This means there were over 1,000 spectators who missed out, in all likelihood due to the problems accessing their tickets.

What frustrated me was the lack of planning by the club. Had they taken the time to invest in back-office and IT systems that would cope with this unique situation, our overall experience as fans would have been much more favourable and those who could attend, would almost certainly have been there.

I felt strongly that those 24 weeks should have been used to prevent something like this - an event I considered foreseeable - from happening. In the end it was all a panic and rush which led to only half a crowd and (though unrelated) a poor performance on the pitch from our team.

Failing to plan is definitely planning to fail, so take some time now to consider where you are at in terms of planning. Do you need to invest more of yourself into this area of your business? Do you need to think about specialist tools? Ask yourself what you would do if a similar situation to that which I've just outlined were to happen. And don't be afraid of the answer. It's better to know now that changes need to be made.

Whatever your point of view, future planning is the only way to future-proof your business and future-proofing your business is the only way to ensure continued and ongoing success.

~ ~ ~ ~

GOAL SETTING ~ WHY IT IS VITAL TO SUCCESS

"To begin with the end in mind means to start with a clear understanding of your destination. It means to know where you're going so that you better understand where you are now and so that the steps you take are always in the right direction."
~ Dr Stephen R Covey

There are numerous books on goal setting and one I would highly recommend is *"The Seven Habits of Highly Effective People"* by *Dr Stephen Covey.* I would then draw your attention to the chapter titled, **Begin With The End In Mind.** This is exactly how we should set goals.

The easiest way for me to explain how to set goals is to use a real-life experience. I am going to talk about a **dream** of mine here, but I want to emphasise that a **dream** is not a **goal.** There's a difference.

My dream had always been to run the London Marathon. I had watched it every year for 23 years and every year I had told myself I would do it. It took every one of those 23 years to make the actual decision to do it. Once I had bitten the bullet and found out the date of the event I was planning to run (18th April 2004), it became a reality, so I reached out to some friends who also shared this dream. Out of ten friends, only two committed, so there were three of us embarking on turning this dream into a reality.

Having never run a marathon before I took the advice of several runners that I knew. It was suggested that I get a decent pair of running shoes and subscribe to Runners World magazine which would help me with my diet and training plan. This, I discovered, was the key.

When I first made the decision to go for it, I was running 3 miles once a week which I knew was never going to be enough to achieve 26 miles in one go barely a year later. This knowledge made me turn to both the Runners World month by month plan and guide, plus Dr Stephen Covey's book. I referred in particular to the chapter I mentioned above - BEGIN WITH THE END IN MIND - so starting at the end (26 miles and the date of the marathon), I worked backwards and figured out what distances I needed to be able to run by what date.

The plan suggested running the longest distance of 18-20 miles four weeks prior to the event. In-between we were to run a number of half marathons and longer distances ranging from 13 to 18 miles in the five to six months leading up to the marathon. I broke this down further to being able to run 10 miles about a month before the first half marathon and then a number of 10K runs (6 miles), 3 months from where I currently was.

These, then were my long and short-term goals. Admittedly, my short-term goal of increasing my distance from 3 to 6 miles in just 12 weeks felt a stretch, but I believed that as I long as I put in the time and commitment to my training, I would get there. And guess what? I did.

Then it was the mid-term goals of 10K runs and half marathons which I made more achievable by entering local events of these distances. This gave me dates to work towards, helped me to keep on track and above all, motivated me.

After that, it was time for the long-term goal, 26 miles on the 18th April 2004. I continued with my training, continued building and when the big day came, successfully completed the dream I had harboured for years.

What had seemed a mammoth task became so much easier and more manageable because I set myself short, mid and long-term goals.

Goal setting in business is no different. Know what you want to achieve in the long-term and then work back from that using your preferred time-scale. As you break it down, build in your mid and then short-term goals so that eventually your task and journey to reach that long-term goal become accessible and easy to achieve.

Try it. Set yourself some business goals: short, mid and long-term.

You'll be amazed at what you can achieve.

~ ~ ~ ~

~ 10 ~

HOW DO YOU EAT AN ELEPHANT?

"It's very difficult to move yourself up bit by bit. It's like trying to eat an elephant. I can do it, it's just I have to do it bite by bite. It's possible. You can eat an elephant, but you have to do it bite by bite. You can't do it all in one go."
~ Dr Stephen R Covey

Running a business – if you are doing it properly – can be overwhelming. There is so much to do to make sure you get it right and there seems to be so little time in which to do which is why you need professional advisors to help you. Not only that, but you need to **remember to take one task at a time.** Like eating an elephant - do it one bite at a time.

Here's how I suggest you organise your tasks:

Take a sheet of A4 paper (or download an online template) and divide it into four. In each section write one of the following:

1. Urgent and Important (Do it now)

2. Not Urgent but Important (Schedule it)

3. Urgent but Not Important (Delegate it)

4. Not Urgent and Not Important (Don't do it)

Now assign each of your tasks to one section. This will help you do the really important stuff first, and don't forget, you can move tasks from one category to another. If you don't have a template like this, *everything* will seem urgent and important.

I remember when I set up *Lionheart Management*, I had an idea of a design for a business card so I made myself an actual sized card with the text and images I thought I wanted. I then carried this around with me for weeks and looked at it regularly. It was one element of my business on which I was unsure so I wanted to get it right before spending money on printing cards, so I gave myself time to make sure I was happy.

There are so many things we need to do when we are starting a business (or review once we have started a business) so it's perfectly understandable to need help.

Don't be frightened to ask for help, and don't try and do everything yourself. Asking for help is a strength in business and not a weakness.

If you don't have an extensive contact base, please ask someone who has. Ask me. I have been networking for over 30 years and pride myself on having a number of trusted reliable contacts from most business sectors.

Also, please remember that it's impossible to start or run a business for **FREE**. You are going to need to spend money on business advice, help and ongoing support so I also suggest using the same template (on the opposite page) to prioritise your spending.

One book that every business owner should read (and re-read regularly) is, *The E Myth Revisited* by *Michael Gerber*. Speak to anyone who has read this book and see how much they value it. Running a business should be fun – or why do it in the first place?

Yes it will be challenging and will test you, but by structuring your business right and by having "experts" you can call on from time to time, you will stay on the right track. And, staying on the right track, greatly increase your chances of success.

It's also important to remember though, that you will not succeed at everything and you will make mistakes. That's okay. It's normal and is the same for every single business owner out there. Mistakes are how we learn and how we improve ourselves and our business. They give us knowledge and strength and provide us with more beneficial information than our successes do. Please, if you take nothing else from this book, remember this.

If you are running a business and have never been networking, I strongly suggest you look into it. Networking and building a trusted circle of advisors and confidantes is what has helped me through the last 33 years of business and enabled me to take it successfully from concept to sale. If you're unsure where to go networking, a quick internet search will help or reach out on platforms such as LinkedIn. Someone will be only too happen to recommend a group you can try.

Remember, you *can* eat an elephant - as crazy as that sounds.

As long as you do it bite by bite.

~ ~ ~ ~

HOW GOOD ARE OUR COMMUNICATION SKILLS?

"The single biggest problem in communication is the illusion that it has taken place." ~ George Bernard Shaw

How good are we at communicating with those we speak to on a regular basis – our families, friends, work colleagues, clients and suppliers?

When you think about it, life is all about communication yet crucially, the part we all miss is this: *it's less about **what** we communicate and more about **how** we communicate.*

Going back a little over 30 years ago when I set up my Advertising Agency, the technology we have today didn't exist. Very few people had mobile phones and those that did carried around an object the size of a house brick complete with detachable aerial.

At that time I didn't know anyone who had 'mobile' phones, web sites or email addresses. The only way we could make appointments was to use local directories or newspapers and make contact via a telephone landline. If we needed to talk to someone then we would either ring the landline number or personally visit them and this held true regardless of who you were communicating with.

I remember going to a networking meeting in those early days and someone handed me their business card which included a website and an email address. Technology was just starting to come to the fore so I really thought they had made it!

We had our first computer in the office in the early 1990's. Mobile phones came some time later so during my first 4 to 5 years in business we had a landline, an A4 diary and a car. It's fair to say that communication was very different back then compared to now. How many people call someone these days as opposed to texting, emailing, or using some other form of online communication? Hardly anyone.

A lot of *families even communicate via the use of technology* rather than face to face. We don't hand write letters any more and electronic cards are used in place of traditional birthday or Christmas greetings, for example. We have all slipped into this way of communicating and personally, I think we need to pull back from it a little. We all get so few cards or letters in the post nowadays that if we do receive a handwritten piece of mail, we appreciate it all the more. This is the same when we, as business owners, use some of the old-fashioned methods of communicating with our customers.

The worldwide pandemic in 2019-2021 highlighted how much we all missed human connection when it was taken from us. We didn't celebrate occasions with family and friends in the same way we did before, nor did we get a hug or handshake from a business colleague acknowledging our achievements. There's no doubt that without technology we would have been completely lost during lock-down. Even on the worst of days we were still able to see and speak to others but what we missed and craved more than anything was that human connection, that physical quality time with family and friends.

I believe now more than ever, that we must put people at the forefront of everything we do. The house we live in and the car we drive are not important. They are objects which are replaceable. Time cannot be regained.

Making sure we are communicating to the absolute best of our abilities is what is important. If we are an employer we need to check-in with our employees on a regular basis and not just around work situations. We need to remember that *every single person is a human being who needs support and kindness from time to time* We never truly know what is going on in another person's life, but we *should at least be treating our staff, colleagues, customers, friends, family as real people, not commodities or statistics*.

Let's have more time for people. Let's not jump to conclusions. We don't know what others are going through at any given time and we cannot possibly control this for them but, what we can do is control our reaction.

We are in complete control of how we react to situations and circumstances so I believe it is key that we commit to becoming better and communicating with everyone in our world.

Let's become communication experts from this point on.

~ ~ ~ ~

~ 12 ~

IF YOU DON'T LOOK FOR IT, YOU WON'T FIND IT

"I know that if you don't look for an alternative, Sophos, you certainly won't find one." ~ Megan Whalen Turner

What are you looking for from life or from your business?

We are all looking for something different but one thing is for sure - if we are not looking we will never find it. Walking through life with our eyes closed can be hugely detrimental, yet so many of us do this day after day.

When you are in business you need to have your eyes wide open all the time. You need to question everything. If you don't and you just go with the flow and do what everyone else does, your chances of success diminish.

Though we could, and should, learn from others, it's down to us to be aware of every element of our business, to understand the alternatives and to explore new ideas. In short, we need to have a positive attitude so that we can spot new opportunities.

Being a business owner requires a totally different level of thinking. It is a tough world out there and we need to stand out from the crowd to succeed. We cannot simply do what everyone else does, nor can we keep doing what we've always done if it isn't working. I remember listening to an Earl Nightingale recording called "The strangest Secret". It was the first ever audio recording of a motivational talk and was produced around the year I was born - 1957. In it Earl said, *"The problem with society today is conformity. Too many people conform. The opposite of courage is not cowardice, it is conformity. They cant think for themselves"*. This is so right and it relates as much today as it did in 1957 - if not more so. It goes to show the principles of success really do not change over the years.

We need to retain the ability to think for ourselves, ask questions and not follow the herd. **We need to work ON ourselves and ON our business which in my experience means spending at least 10% of our time ON ourselves and ON our business.** This is a great habit to get into.

~ ~ ~ ~

~ 13 ~

JUST HOW IMPORTANT IS RESPECT?

"Treat people the way you want to be treated. Talk to people the way you want to be talked to. Respect is earned, not given."
~ Hussein Nishah

The Gerard Butler movie *Law Abiding Citizen*, dedicates much of its plot line to respect. If you are familiar with the movie, you'll know what I'm talking about. It's a great movie that illustrates just how important respect is.

The thing about respect, though, is that it has to be earned. It can't be demanded and it's definitely a two-way street. In order for us to get respect from others, we have to show respect to them and (as in so many things in life) we have to give before we receive.

Respect starts from an early age. As parents or teachers or guardians, we have a responsibility to respect our children and through our actions, show them what it is to respect those around them. It isn't taught simply to help them make their way down one side of that two-way street though, it's also for their own development and resilience. In my experience, those who have never been taught respect and/or have little to no *self*-respect, will never be able to show respect to others.

Respect is also one of those funny little words that we all say, but perhaps don't fully understand the gravity of. The quote at the top of this article is, I think, a great way to define respect and learning this from an early age will have a massive impact on who we become in life and the kinds of people we go on to be as adults. I am sure I'm not alone in witnessing many parental interactions, or interactions with bosses or persons in power, where they have demanded *our* respect without first/also giving *us the courtesy of theirs*. One thing I can tell you about people like this is that they will never be leaders. Not only do they lack one of the most fundamental life skills, their lack of respect for everyone around them pushes others away until often, they end up alone.

In my 68 years of life I have witnessed a marked difference in respect now, to how it was when I was growing up. So many people today seem to take the respect of others for granted without giving any in return.

One of my biggest bugbears are those who do not respect the time and money of others which is something I've seen in many encounters over the years. These are the kinds of people who will make an appointment at a customers home and then fail to turn up, or will turn up several hours late without even so much as a phone call. This is totally disrespectful and the damage from overlooking the importance of keeping the customer in the loop can be huge. They are almost certainly at risk of losing a great deal of business to those who do turn up on time.

The same can be said for money. Don't disrespect other's money, and by this I am alluding to not overcharging your customers. Though you may have a short-term win by doing this, it will in the long run lead to reputational damage. Similarly, if you owe someone money pay it back and pay it back on time. Do not use excuses. Its the easiest way to lose friends.

Respect might only be a little word, but it can make a massive difference in so many ways. Here are seven actions you can take in your daily life to show and practice respect:

1. Listen and be present. We have two ears and one mouth for a reason.
2. Be thoughtful of others' feelings. Don't think only of yourself.
3. Acknowledge kindness and say thank you. It's such an easy way to put a smile on someone's face.
4. Address mistakes with goodwill. Don't cover them up. Be honest and you will win big time.
5. Make decisions based on *what* is right and not *who* you like.
6. Respect physical boundaries. If you're not sure where these are, err on the side of caution.
7. Live and let live.

Being continuously aware of the need to give respect is one of the major building blocks of a successful life and business.

When we are respectful it makes us feel good about ourselves and, more importantly, it helps others to feel good about themselves (and us), too.

~ ~ ~ ~

~ 14 ~

READERS ARE LEADERS

"Not all readers are leaders, but all leaders are readers."
~ Harry S Truman

I am sure we have all seen or heard this quote and in my opinion it is very true. It does not mean that you won't succeed if you don't read personal development books, but your chances of success and of building a better business are that much greater.

Everyone I know personally who has a successful business spends time and money working on themselves and growing their knowledge through relevant industry and development books. It doesn't matter how you access books - many prefer audiobook format now - the important thing is that you *are* accessing the information.

Just because we are business 'owners', it doesn't mean we automatically know how to run a business. I know many who have a company with a large number of staff, but have no idea how to manage people, usually because they don't know how to run a business and have not taken the appropriate actions to learn.

Often, these business owners believe that they already know everything and are reticent to accept advice or help. They will try to be all things to all people and it is easy to tell that they don't spend time reading any kind of business books. If I recommend that they do, usually they will scoff. Their mentality is that *'they own a business (which may or may not be doing well) and therefore/regardless they don't need any help'*. When I meet these kinds of people, my response is simply to let them 'crack on'. I am not going to change their mindset and nor do I want to waste time trying.

I know from experience that 'true' leaders are those who read (beneficial content) daily and will continuously educate themselves. True leaders are always looking to learn from others, readily take advice and are humble. As a result they will have a great team of people around them - both staff and outsourced - and they know how to manage and get the best out of everyone they work with.

In addition, successful leaders understand the difference between a cost and an investment which allows them to have great businesses, not only financially but in so many other ways.

From my own perspective, I thought that once I left school at 16, that was the end of my education. I was now in the big wide world of earning, not learning. My first job was in a bank and shortly after I joined I was told I would need to attend college twice a week to study for banking exams in order to progress. That job only last 4 years and by the time I left at the age of 20, I had a shit attitude and thought I knew everything. Then at 21, I met my wife Denise, got into network marketing at the age of 23 which led me to a personal development programme, and that was when I really started to understand the power this had.

I began hanging around with successful or success minded people; people who believed in me. I read personal development books, listened to motivational, inspirational teaching tapes and CD's and attended monthly motivational seminars - all by choice.

Is it any wonder then, that by the time I started my first conventional business at the age of 30, I understood how to build one successfully?

So, to the crux of this article, *do readers make the best leaders?* Without any doubt in my mind they do. If you don't read personal development books, I would strongly suggest you start now.

Remember the choices we make today will have a big influence on who we become tomorrow.

~ ~ ~ ~

~ 15 ~

SIMPLE ACTS OF KINDNESS ~ HOW THEY HELP US ALL

"No act of kindness, no matter how small, is ever wasted."
~ Aesop

We have all heard about performing *simple acts of kindness*, but how many of us understand their power and moreover, do it with regularity?

Simple acts of kindness don't need to cost money, they just need to put a smile on someone's face, and make them feel better about themselves. Many of us are struggling mentally, a circumstance not helped by the recent COVID-19 pandemic, so it's worth remembering that performing a *simple act of kindness* often takes little effort but can generate huge rewards.

We have a basic human need to feel good about ourselves. When we don't, our lives and the lives of those around us suffer. We become less productive, we stop showing up for our friends and family, we may become slack when it comes to work ... none of which is our fault, these (and many more) are symptoms of how we are feeling. Which, if we're not feeling great about ourselves, is not good.

It's tough to keep a positive mindset at times. It takes extra effort which we may not have, all of which leads to what feels like a never-ending downward spiral. If, when we are feeling this way, we are the recipient of *simple acts of kindness* **from others, they can really help support us** when we are at our lowest. Conversely, it's important that we recognise the **benefit of giving these simple acts, too.**

So what are some simple acts of kindness we can do?

- Greet someone kindly when you are out on a walk.
- Knock on a neighbours door to make sure they are okay.
- Give someone a call or drop them a message to let them know you are thinking about them.
- Offer to make that very British cup of tea for family members or friends.
- Lend a fellow business owner a book you've found hugely beneficial.

I could go on, but you get the idea.

None of these suggestions cost a penny, yet they will mean more than money can buy to those in receipt. It really does cost nothing to be polite and courteous, so why not practice it more?

I was given *"The Happiest Man on Earth"* which is a book written by *Eddie Jaku* who is an Auschwitz survivor. Even though he was going through hell, Eddie was kind to everyone and helped out his fellow prisoners whenever he could. For Eddie, being kind gave him a focus and was instrumental in him surviving the horrors of Auschwitz and for those around him, his kindness lifted them during the atrocities of a time we cannot even begin to comprehend.

To be successful in whatever it is we are striving for in life we have to have a positive mindset. If we extend that mindset to others, it's amazing how much that positivity can benefit them, too. It's a bit like when we talked about respect in a previous article. If we give, then we receive, even if it's not immediate or financially motivated. The feeling of knowing we have made someone's day just that little bit better, is priceless.

If you want to up the ante then buy someone a gift, send them some flowers, or buy the coffee for the person behind you in the queue. The great thing about modern technology is that you can gift anonymously if you don't want your identity to be known. It's just about showing someone that you care - it's not about thanks or gratitude. *You should offer simple acts of kindness for one reason and one reason only: because you can.*

When we perform these acts of kindness, it is often the case that our recipient will do the same for someone else. If we can help to keep this momentum going then that can only be a good thing. Simple acts of kindness really are simple, all they require is little extra effort on our part which, when measured against the happiness they create, can only ever be worthwhile.

It is also a great habit to get into as a small business owner. We can assist others to achieve more in their businesses by helping them feel better about themselves. *All it takes is one simple act of kindness.*

~ ~ ~ ~

~ 16 ~

THE BATTLE SCARS OF BUSINESS OWNERSHIP

"I think scars are like battle wounds - beautiful in a way. They show what you've been through and how strong you are for coming out of it."
~ Demi Lovato

It's been 38 years now since I set up business in September of 1987. Six years prior to that I·had first been introduced to a **personal development programme** (referenced in previous articles), which meant I felt I was in a good place to set out on my own. I was prepared.

Through networking I had met some very successful people who had set up an Advertising business and were looking for "Agents" to help them grow the business. A colleague and I seized this **opportunity** each buying a distributorship in adjoining areas. Though we were inexperienced in Advertising, we were not new to sales and embraced knocking on doors to sell advertising space.

The first real challenge came at the end of 1988. We were £24k in debt (about £75k today) and as we'd only been going for a year, we needed to carefully consider our next steps. It was only through the graces of the local Bank Manager that we had made it this far (agreeing to extend our overdraft), which meant we were going to have to face up to a massive **change**. The fact we were able to do this illustrates the importance of **relationships** and **trust**. The Bank **trusted** that we would repay our debt and wouldn't shirk our **responsibility** to do so.

Having **strong work ethics, strong core values** and a **high moral standard** was something both myself and my business partner shared. When a situation arose where we couldn't deliver what a client had paid for (due to factors outside of our control) we took the decision to offer this client a full refund. He accepted whilst also stating that in his 30 years of business, no one else had ever offered him a full refund. This confirmed that our action at that time was the right one.

At the back end of 1989, the company which was our main supporter folded leaving us very much in the lurch. Everything we had relied on them so we faced another **choice**: did we go back to working for someone else?

We had already had 2 years of **freedom** so this was never an option, instead we doubled-down on our business and looked for new **opportunities**. By that time we both understood we needed to grasp every **opportunity** that came our way and soon we were offered a chance to work in the **outdoor** advertising space. In the two previous years we had learned so much as well as experienced both **success** and **failure** and were keen to hit the ground running with this new opportunity.

I began **networking** and discovered just how much help and support was out there. I started to understand *how* to build a **better business** and realised I could not be all things to all people - it just wasn't possible. Networking allowed me to meet others with different skill sets (accountants, HR, business coaches etc.) which meant I could start **outsourcing** parts of the business. Outsourcing is covered in a previous article, but what you need to understand for the purposes of business ownership is the i**mportance of outsourcing**.

The other thing to remember is that **people buy from people** so building relationships whilst networking is key to your ongoing success. Some I networked with in the early days, remain great friends and business contacts.

It's fair to say that, though we had our ups and downs, once we began to **understand how to build our business**, it went from strength to strength. Those we worked with **trusted** and **respected** us and we **reciprocated**. It really is all about **relationships**.

I was clear in my long term goal that I wanted to have sold the business by the time I was 60, which meant a lot of early **planning**. You can never plan too early, and this opened us up to the opportunity of buying a couple of properties for rental income. We were **diversifying**. That property portfolio grew to a total of 23 over the years, which is what went on to become my pension fund.

With all of the technological advances and changes in the advertising industry, it became apparent we would need to **adapt** some of our practices and embrace areas like websites. This is where my business partner and I parted company as our goals began to differ. Moving forward with technology helped me survive three recessions and learn how to **not overspend**, **build a team** and **delegate**.

Finally, after 33 years I achieved my planned exit strategy and sold the business. Every word in **bold** in this article underpin the key lessons I learned and the most important thing to remember is this:

Business is all about relationships. You can't be successful on your own.

~ ~ ~ ~

~ 17 ~

LIFE IS BUILT ON THIN THREADS

*"When you feel that there is only a thin thread of hope, it is really not
a thread but a massive connecting link."*
~ Elder Richard G. Scott

People do not cross our paths by accident - it happens for a reason. Life is built on so many thin threads, so many things that just as easily could not have happened. This is something I firmly believe.

Think back to events in your lives. How you met your life partner, how you started your business, how certain events came about and I am sure you will believe this, too.

Let me illustrate with a potted history of thin threads which have run through my life:

- I met my wife in 1979. She was instrumental in me starting my business.
- How we met - that's a thin thread.
- How our relationship developed - another thin thread.
- The location of our first house - one more thin thread.

But here's the thing:

- Within months of moving into our first house we met a couple through my wife's party plan venture (thin thread).
- This couple lived two streets away and became good friends (thin thread).
- Barry ended up becoming my business partner (thin thread).
- Barry then introduced me to another couple (thin thread) ...
- ... who introduced me to a network marketing business (thin thread) ...
- ... which was instrumental in the formation of my Advertising Agency.
- This was also where I was introduced to the personal development programme which gave me a solid foundation on which to build my business (thin thread).

Of course, every thin thread relies on us being proactive and following its journey but there is no doubt that they are there for all of us, we just need to look and learn to explore them.

Our minds are very complex. We will never understand exactly how they work and how events in our lives happen. They just do and it's my belief that this is how life works.

Pretty much every strong relationship I have with those I spend so much of my time with - in my personal and business life - all have their own stories of thin threads that led us to meet.

As I've mentioned in previous articles, relationships are so important to our business and to the people we become so we need to choose wisely.

Follow every thin thread but be aware that you may occasionally find an imposter wrapped in tin foil instead of a Knight in shining armour.

Perhaps take a few moments now to reflect on some of your key life events and identify the thin threads that have led you to them. I promise, they're there.

~ ~ ~ ~

~ 18 ~

WHAT CAN WE LEARN FROM GARETH SOUTHGATE?

"We need diversity of thought in the world to face the new challenges."
~ Tim Berners-Lee

If you are British, you will almost certainly have heard of Gareth Southgate. As (former) coach of the England football team he has been the subject of many articles in recent times, often in reference to the people he surrounds himself with. Gareth has achieved a significant level of success with the England football team which comes not only from his skills, but also from those he's had around him. What Gareth has done, to great effect, is build a team of experts who are **experts in their field**, as opposed to being experts in football. According to every article I have read, Gareth Southgate understands that to be successful and build a successful team, he needs to add diversity and incorporate people who *think the same* but *approach it from different angles.*

A fantastic quote I read in a *BBC* article by *Matthew Syed* states:

"If there is one universal truth about human psychology, it is that we love being surrounded by people who think just like us."

The Ancient Greeks referred to this as "homophily" which means "love of the same".

Plato is credited for observing that "birds of a feather, flock together" and, if you think about, this is spot on. A big part of our success comes from those around us so if we want to achieve a particular goal, it makes sense to spend time with successful or success minded people.

You do not build success by having a team who all come from the same sector. You need views from others who are not "blinkered" and who see things differently. Gareth knew that just by building a support team of footballing people was not going to give him what he wanted - it had been done for over 50 years without any continued success.

This problem as we know does not just apply to English football. Many large corporates believe that by hiring the best people in their particular sector will give continued success yet often, all it does is give more of the same. We need people who think differently to ourselves and each other so that we can explore opposing viewpoints. We need people who are creative to think outside of the box. People who are routinely driven to provide stability and order. People who are all about the minutest detail to prevent us from making too many mistakes. And whilst these people may well be present in our given industry, chances are they aren't, because as we've just learned from Plato, *'birds of a feather, flock together'*.

It's all about bringing in people who have the right attitude and great relationship skills in my opinion. You can teach them your industry, but you cannot teach the difference in perspectives and un-blinkered thinking they will bring.

Gareth Southgate once said, *"I like listening to people who know things that I don't. That's how you learn"*.

He's right. Just because we may own and run the business does not mean we have all the answers. We need to be humble enough to learn from others.

There are classic examples of companies who remained set in their ways to their eventual detriment, simply because decision makers were all of the same ilk. Blockbuster Video missed opportunities available due to the growth of the internet and continued on as they had always done. They went from dominating the movie rental business to bankruptcy. Kodak is another example. They were so fixated on print photography that they didn't maximise opportunities afforded by digital.

Though Gareth and his team did not win the Euros, under his leadership they achieved more success than with most previous managers. What I think we can all take from this is that it pays to think outside of the box and go against the grain. Having a team around us who all know the same things, will only limit our business growth and opportunities.

Diversity in everything is so important.

Success in business and sport is really not a million miles apart.

~ ~ ~ ~

~ 19 ~

WHAT DID I LEARN? ~ MY FIRST TWO YEARS IN BUSINESS

*"There is only one thing more painful than learning from experience,
and that is not learning from experience."*
~ *Archibald MacLeish*

What *did* I learn in my first two years in business - and how can that help you?

As mentioned in other articles, I became involved in network marketing in 1982, which led to the personal development programme I have also previously referred to. I think, if I could give you only one piece of advice it would be that. Find yourself a similar programme or engage a mentor. Someone who believes in you and helps to guide you is invaluable, regardless of how long you've been in business.

Five years later I started my Advertising business on September 4th 1987, with no money. Through my networking contacts I was able to form the business and buy a distributorship in digital advertising. It was very much a 'Del Boy' moment as myself and my business partner moved into a completely new service and arena. Digital marketing was unproven and my wife was pregnant with our first daughter; what the heck was I thinking?

Though I had a business partner (which again is something I would recommend you seriously consider), we had little to no capital and made ends meet by using our bank overdraft. At the end of the first 12 months, we were £24,000 in debt. Obviously, this is not the best way to fund a business and would probably not work today, but the lesson here is to really think about funding - how much you need, how much you want to have ongoing and how you are going to get it. Nowadays there are community options such as crowd funding or sponsorship which can be worthwhile, too.

At the end of our first year we were selling enough digital advertising space, but we were struggling to get renewals, which meant reviewing our target market and charging structure. Tweaking these led to a better second year, however the Franchisor (for want of a better word) went bust leaving us with a business that was starting to work but no one to master and produce the adverts we were busily selling.

As luck would have it, one of our customers was a local bus operator who said they had a couple of large poster advertising spaces available if we wanted them. With little choice we didn't hesitate and grabbed at the opportunity. This, though, was a different service to the one we had been working previously, so my business partner and I set about learning everything we could about the outdoor advertising industry. In less than 3 months we knew pretty much all we needed to know and were able to turn that business into a £1 million + a year business over a 33 year period. For the last 12 years I ran the business on my own, but by then I had built a great team around me, many of whom remained with the business once I sold it.

Key lessons:

- Don't try and be all things to all people.
- Do what you are good at and outsource everything else.
- Don't employ people without the help of a professional HR person.
- Make sure you have IT support in place.
- Get a book-keeper to do the accounts.
- Keep a check on costs.
- Know how profitable each service is you sell - how much are your overheads each month? Are you making money?
- Review costs regularly.
- Put systems and processes in place.

Most business owners have no idea how to run a business properly, or if they do, they still try and do it all themselves. They think if they are working 70 or 80 hours a week that they have a good business - they don't. Its about balance. A great way to think about your business is to run it as if you were planning to franchise it. Just that simple shift in mindset produces a huge amount of clarity.

Planning is also key. You might not have an exit strategy when you start out, but you should definitely have a long-term plan with that in mind. Your plan will adjust so you need to adapt and change with the times.

No one teaches us how to run a business. To do it properly takes trust in someone (that mentor I have referenced many times) who we can follow and who will guide us along the way. Mentors have been there, done it and got the T-shirt, so they are ideally placed to support new and established businesses alike.

As I said at the start of this piece, if I could give you only one piece of advice it would be this: engage the right mentor.

~ ~ ~ ~

~ 20 ~

WHEEL OF LIFE

"There are many spokes on the wheel of life. First, we are here to explore new possibilities." ~ Ray Charles

It is important to have good balance in your life and however many segments there are, they should be pretty equal. Now I am sure we all strive for this, but so many of us are imbalanced. If we divided our lives into segments I doubt they would be perfectly equal, which causes many issues in both our personal and business worlds.

When we are born all of our time is ours, and as we get older, our parents tend to fill these segments for us, with sports or other social activities, education, family time, spiritual time and so on. Once we start work, this is where I think the imbalance really starts to happen. We may have a pushy boss who expects more and more from us and although we signed a contract to work 40 hours a week, in so many cases we are expected to work more.

In the same way that if we run our own business, we might think that if we work more we will have/achieve more, yet that is rarely the case. I never looked at my 38 years of running businesses like that because I wanted to maintain balance in my life. Even during the most challenging of times, I tried to keep to a maximum of 50 hours per week and aimed to keep weekends free for my family. We also endeavoured to take holidays so that I could spend quality time with my wife and daughters.

Sadly I've met so many business owners who think it's perfectly okay to work 70-80 hours per week. It's even more concerning when they seem proud of this which is something I've never understood. To my mind, if you're having to work over and above 50 hours per week (which in itself is above the Government recommended working week of 48 hours), then I would suggest you really need to take a long hard look at your business model. Of course it's important to invest time in your business but there really should be a balance between this and your downtime, otherwise you'll struggle to maintain either.

Since the end of March 2020 and throughout the pandemic, we were all forced to re-evaluate our lives and look at how we were spending our time. Some people made life-changing decisions whilst others will have made the necessary adjustments at the time, but returned almost instantly to their previous habits when able. The thing is, the support is out there to help us maintain an improved balance, so my message to you as a business owner is to remember to ask for help. The support throughout the small business community is better than I have ever seen it (certainly in the networking world) and I am incredibly proud to be a small part of that.

I get disturbed when I read reports stating that some people worked longer hours than ever during lock-down - which doesn't feel right to me at all. Just because we're working from home, doesn't mean we have to work every hour available to us, in fact, if we are able to exercise discipline, we will arguably have less distractions than when we're in the office.

We also need to be spending more time on Mental Health and Education. I can't stress enough how important it is to look after ourselves and make sure we keep mentally and physically fit. I find it hugely beneficial to take time away from the computer every day - even if only for a few minutes. Using that time to get a bit of exercise, like going for a short walk, will have such a positive impact on how we are feeling both mentally and physically.

I also advocate spending time on personal development; learning soft skills such as improved communication and listening as well as more specialist subjects which may be relative purely to your industry. Learning is key to becoming an improved version of ourselves and one who is better able to manage the inevitable ups and downs of life as a business owner.

We should all enrich our lives as much as we can. Take time to stop and look at nature, for example, or to help others, or to be with our families. When we leave this world, no one remembers the car we drove or the house we lived in.

What we are remembered for is how many lives we touched.

~ ~ ~ ~

2 Section Two

Me & My Business
You & Your Business

21.   WHERE DID IT ALL START? ~ PERSONAL DEVELOPMENT

22.   ARE WE REALLY ALL IN THE SAME BOAT?

23.   BE THE HERO OF YOUR OWN STORY

24.   ARE YOU STUCK IN THE MAZE?

25.   DO YOU HAVE A SINGLE-MINDED ATTITUDE TO LIFE?

26.   EMBRACE LIFE'S EXPERIENCES - THEY SHAPE US

27.   HAVE YOU EVER SAID, 'IT'S NOT FAIR!'?

28.   JUST WORKING HARD - IS IT ENOUGH?

29.   TAKING RESPONSIBILITY IN EVERYTHING YOU DO

30.   THEORY OR EXPERIENCE?

31.   WE HAVE TO LIVE WITH THE CHOICES WE MAKE

32.   WHAT IS YOUR WHY?

33.   WHAT MAKES US WHO WE ARE?

34.   WHAT MAKES US STAND OUT FROM THE CROWD?

35.   YOU ARE THE PROBLEM TO YOUR PROBLEMS

36.   YOU ARE WHAT YOU DO - ACTION!

~ 21 ~

WHERE DID IT ALL START? ~ PERSONAL DEVELOPMENT

"Daily habits are the key to success." ~ Jim Rohn

I left school at 16 to start working in a bank because mum suggested it. *"You're good with figures, why don't you work in a bank?"* She said. As I didn't really know what I wanted to do, it seemed as good a choice as any and as far as I was concerned, my education was over. I wanted to earn money. I was onto the next chapter in my life.

I stayed at the bank for four years during which time I began working towards my banking exams. In order to progress, I was told this was necessary so for two nights a week I would travel some distance to evening college. Having thought my time in education was over, I'd somehow ended up right back there, yet astonishingly, it took me four years to realise I hated doing exams. Subsequently I left the bank and went to work at Heathrow Airport where there were no more exams, just 'on the job' learning.

I got married at the age of twenty-three to my wonderful wife Denise and we started our new life together in our first home. We began to make new friends with people of a similar age and it was through these friends that we were introduced to a Network Marketing business. This happy accident, it turned out, was the best thing that ever happened to me in my working life.

It was during this time that someone imparted a piece of wisdom. They told me that, *'in five years time we will be exactly the same person as we are today, with the exception of those we mix with and the books we read.'*

Through the network marketing business I started to educate myself on how to work with people, how to build relationships with people, how to be successful, how to have a dream etc., all of which I did by reading books. To my surprise I began devouring these books and I still do so today. I also made sure to hang around with successful or success minded people and it began to rub off – big time.

The thing about books that I hadn't appreciated at school, was that you need to read the right books in order to learn. When I figured this out, I started reading a new book every month on how to build a successful business or how to build relationships. These were known as PMA books (Positive Motivational Attitude) and included business books as well as those dedicated to motivation and inspirational ideas.

When the opportunity arose to start my own conventional business in 1987, I jumped at the chance. With all my reading and research over the previous seven years, I genuinely believed I was ready to put my learnings into practice.

To cut a long story short, I built that business over the next thirty years - which was not without its challenges - but in 2016 I was able to sell on a well-established and successful company and achieve a three-year earn out which ended in March of 2019.

Since then I've been able to pass my knowledge and experience onto other small business owners, primarily because I did the groundwork in the early years. I made sure I was ready and learned everything I could before I took that leap.

Most small business owners start their companies with an idea, or perhaps they have been made redundant, or have some spare cash to invest, or are fed up of working for someone else.

Whatever the catalyst, I know from first-hand experience that you need help to build a business. It's so true when people tell you that '*you don't know what you don't know*' and that '*you don't know who you don't know*'.

There are a lot of good people out there who will help you. There are also a lot of people who will take your money and not give you anything in return.
Be careful of your knight in shining armour as it could be an imposter wrapped in tin foil.

Without a shadow of a doubt, personal development is vital. If you are running a business and don't read personal development books – here is a tip. **Start now.**

You may not know it but take it from me, it will make you a better business person and you will be far more successful with this knowledge than you will ever be without it.

~ ~ ~ ~

~ 22 ~

ARE WE *REALLY* ALL IN THE SAME BOAT?

"We may be in the same storm, but we are not all in the same boat."
~ Unknown (facebook.com/love.peace.inity.respect)

Let's set the scene – three owners decide to take their boats out to sea. The weather when they set out was fine and the forecast looked good. It had been good all summer. Then an unexpected storm came in. What happened to each of these boats?

Boat Number One: This boat had been worked on tirelessly by the owners every year to make sure it was in tip top condition. They updated it with the latest technology to ensure its seaworthiness and incorporated every safety feature they could. The boat was balanced, fitted with the market leading buoyancy aids and comfortable for its occupants. The owners liked to spend time on the boat but were always prepared for the worst. They wanted to make sure (to the best of their ability) that everyone on board remained safe.

Boat Number Two: This boat had work done now and again, mainly when the owners could be bothered. Though there was technology on board it wasn't the best - about five years out of date - but they were reassured by the fact that they at least had some technological aids. The boat broke down from time to time and the owners would patch it up, promising to give it a full overhaul one day. The buoyancy aids on board were a bit like the technology - okay, but not the best - however the owners rationalised that as it was usually only themselves on board, it was fine for things to be a little out of date. Though they did obviously care about the safety of friends and family who used the boat, again they were comfortable that the measures they had in place were sufficient.

Boat Number Three: This boat was in really poor condition. It never had any work done on it, in fact, the owners didn't even lift it onto a dry dock to check that the hull remained seaworthy. Any technology they had fitted was minimal and largely didn't work, and buoyancy aids were non-existent but the owners rationalised that they only ever took the boat out in good weather, so they didn't need to worry too much. They always checked the weather before a trip (which was the only preparation they did), and felt this was more than adequate. If the weather looked rough they didn't go out; in any case, no one ever wanted to accompany them. It was as simple as that.

The storm that these three boats encountered was unexpected. Each crew believed they were sailing on a good day weather-wise, so they had to make adjustments to their plans. The main focus was to return to the harbour safely. Here's what happened:

Boat Number One: The passengers didn't panic. Using their up to date technology they were easily able to reach the coastguard who assisted them in navigating their way safely back to harbour. Due to its comfort and stability, everyone remained safe and uninjured and there was no damage to the boat. Although it had been a frightening experience, their meticulous work and preparations meant that any impact to all on board was minimised.

Boat Number Two: They were in a bit of trouble. Unfortunately their outdated technology made reaching the coastguard nigh on impossible so they had to ride out the worst of the storm. The boat was thrown from side to side causing injuries to everyone on board. It was pure luck that they were able to make it back to the harbour, though all its occupants were incredibly shaken as well as injured. The boat also suffered significant damage which the owners didn't have the funds to repair but more importantly, the whole experience caused rift between the friends which turned out to be too large to heal. The owners lost their boat and they lost their friends.

Boat Number Three: Due to their lack of care, even the basic radio on this boat didn't work. Unable to contact anyone for help, boat number three never made it back to the harbour. As it continued to take on water, the terrified occupants huddled together - until, by a sheer stroke of good fortune, they were rescued by a passing coastguard vessel which had been deployed to seek out any boats in trouble. Minutes after their rescue, boat number three became a victim of the yawning sea. The owners were traumatised by their ordeal and were never able to afford another boat - even if they'd wanted to. All they would say when questioned was: "If we had spent more time looking after our boat, none of this would have happened."

Do you recognise your business here?

Which boat are you in?

To be fair, whichever boat you are in it's imperative to reach out to others for help and support - but it becomes critical if your business is a passenger in **boats two** and **three**.

Don't watch your business sink. There's no guarantee you'll be fortunate enough to be rescued.

~ ~ ~ ~

~ 23 ~

BE THE HERO OF YOUR OWN STORY

*"A hero is an ordinary individual who finds the strength to persevere
and endure in spite of overwhelming obstacles."*
~ Christopher Reeve

Whilst watching a CIA thriller some time ago, one of the actors delivered the following line:

"Be the hero of your own story."

This gave me pause. It seems so obvious and yet, are we all actually our own heroes? What are we doing to make sure of this?

Reflecting, the answer to this question for me is in my children. I have two daughters who I've been proud to support through my own business since the day they were born. That's not to say it's been easy, far from it, but neither of my daughters has ever seen me work for someone else which means I've always been the author of my own story. I guess it's a bit of a cliché, but I always wanted to be a hero to my kids and I wanted to earn that title, so every decision I made and every day I worked, I had them at the forefront of my mind. Sure, they could find heroes in pop stars and fictitious characters, but I wanted more than that for them. This testimonial from my eldest daughter, Lauren, posted on my website in 2011, (www.lionheartmanagement.co.uk), truly means everything.

> *"Being Richard's daughter, I know exactly the type of person that he is! My dad has definitely influenced me in many ways. He is a positive person who always puts other people first. Having achieved so much in life, he is definitely someone that I look up to and I hope that one day I can be as successful as he is".*

My driving force over the last 40 years has always been my kids and, if just a small portion of what I've learned and experienced can be passed onto them, then it will all have been worth it.

I am going to have a 'proud dad' moment now, though, because both of my daughters have grown up to be extraordinarily strong, successful, independent women who have strong morals and values and who always put others first. I

64

cannot, nor do I wish to take credit for all of this, but I hope that by showing them how to overcome obstacles, how to be creative and to think outside of the box and most importantly, how to be kind to others, I have in some small way contributed to the people they are today.

I want you to take a moment here to think about the obstacles that you have overcome - both in business and personally. Have you been able to learn from these? Have you been true to yourself and your values and continued to maintain your own narrative?

I believe we are all ordinary people who do extraordinary things to succeed in life. We are regularly overcoming obstacles along the way and it is *how* we overcome these that will rub off on those around us.

I've said it in many of these articles, but if you are unsure how to cope with your business obstacles, then don't be afraid to ask for help. Asking for help is actually a sign of strength, not weakness and if you can show this to your children, imagine how balanced they will be as they mature.

Being the hero of your own story is critical. We shouldn't let anyone else narrate our journey because it is OUR journey, not theirs. If we can do this and remain true to ourselves and our values, whatever we leave behind as our legacy will have way more value than any amount of money.

Sometimes it's easy to use our kids as an excuse for not doing things (too busy, don't have time etc.), however I flipped that on its head and instead, made them my *entire reason* for doing what I did.

I'm not saying I'm right (or wrong) here, but what is *important* is that we all have a *reason for doing what we are doing*. A reason that is *ours* and *ours alone*.

Be a hero to your kids.

Be a hero to yourself.

No one else deserves to be that person.

~ ~ ~ ~

~ 24 ~

ARE YOU STUCK IN THE MAZE?

"If our core belief is based on what other people think, then we eventually will allow their opinions to become our reality."
~ Darren Johnson

Do you feel like you are going round and around the maze and there is no way out? If you are answering 'yes' to this, then it could be time to take a look at your beliefs. Beliefs are hugely powerful. More powerful than most of us give them credit for. They have the power to hold us back to the point of crippling us, or move us forward to the point of limitless success.

Self-limiting beliefs are the worst. Though they exist purely in our minds, they wield so much power as to effectively imprison us.

Dr Spencer Johnson is the inspiration for this article. If you have never read his books, *"Who Moved My Cheese"* or the follow up *"Out of the Maze"*, then I highly recommend that you do.

According to Andrea Pearce[1] from the Open University, self-limiting beliefs:

> *"Often take the form of inner mind chatter that is negative and self-sabotaging, such as 'I'll never be able to do that' or 'I'm not ready' or 'I'm not good enough'. These become mental habits repeating in an endless loop, leading us to doubt our capabilities, and that our goals and dreams are impossible to achieve. This can deceive us into thinking we are less than we are."*

What psychologists have come to understand is that if we **accept a limiting belief**, then it **becomes a truth** for us. This then perpetuates the strength of the belief, even though it is almost certainly untrue.

Self-limiting beliefs often form the walls of our comfort zone. The challenge is that when we get stuck in our comfort zone, it becomes increasingly difficult to think outside of this. To challenge those self-beliefs. What, though, if we knew that by challenging these beliefs, we would be able to initiate major changes in our lives?

---

1 https://www.open.edu/openlearn/health-sports-psychology/psychology/reframing-self-limiting-beliefs

I ask every business owner I work with to consider the 'what if' question. For example:

~ What if I believed I could increase my turnover by 10%?
~ What if I believed that my product was revolutionary?
~ What if I believed I would be able to expand my business?

Whatever their concern - or self-limiting belief - I ask them to add 'what if' to the front of it and turn it around. Instead of saying 'I can't', how about saying 'I can'.

If you think about being in a maze - perhaps you've been in it for what feels like hours and you've tried every possible way out, to the point where you feel like giving up. The reality is, there is a way out. There is always a way out of every maze (some believe you keep turning right!), so instead of thinking, "I can't get out", how about believing that you "can get out". You're not going to be any worse off for changing this thought pattern and chances are, you will absolutely find the exit.

What about trying a new belief? If you change a belief, does that change you?

> *"A belief is a thought that you trust is true; it does not make it true,*
> *but it does hold you prisoner."*
> ~ *Dr Spencer Johnson*

We don't like it when someone challenges our beliefs. We feel offended when anyone suggests that what we are thinking may not be true. We resist changing our minds because we feel threatened. We don't want to change our beliefs because we like them. It feels safe. Yet, choosing a new belief can be energising.

> *"You are not your belief. You are the person who chooses your beliefs."*
> ~ *Dr Spencer Johnson*

- Notice your beliefs ~ remember they are only thoughts that you trust are true.
- Don't believe everything you think ~ sometimes 'facts' are just how *you* see things.
- Let go of what isn't working ~ you can't launch a new quest with old baggage.
- Look outside the maze ~ consider the unlikely; explore the impossible.
- Choose a new belief ~ changing what you think does not change who you are.
- There are no limits to what you *can* believe ~ you *can* do, enjoy and experience way more than you think.

~ 25 ~

DO YOU HAVE A SINGLE-MINDED ATTITUDE TO LIFE?

*"An attitude to life which seeks fulfilment in the single-minded pursuit
of wealth - in short, materialism - does not fit into this world because
it contains within itself no limiting principle, while the environment
in which it's placed is strictly limited."*
~ E F Schumacher

Are you single-minded? It's a tough one because on the one hand, we need to have a single-minded devotion to our goal in order to achieve our mission in life but, at what detrimental cost does this single-mindedness come? Does it, for example, negatively affect our friends and family?

It is easy to see how we can become obsessively single-minded when it comes to building wealth. There are many millionaires and billionaires who have built empires through pursuing their goals (to the exception of all else), however, I'm not a lover of employing a single-minded attitude just to build wealth. In most cases, in my experience, this way of being can lead to us forgetting what is really important.

In the early days of my business, I was given the following piece of advice:

*"Don't worry about making money. Build strong relationships and as
long as you have a product or service in demand, money will flow."*

This has absolutely been the result. Perhaps money has not always flowed as much as I wished when in a mindset of financial abundance, however the wealth of friends and business colleagues I have built up over the last 40 + years, for me, far outweighs the financial rewards.

During the COVID-19 pandemic, many of us were forced to re-evaluate our lives and consider what - or who - really mattered. Though the financial burden was great and many are still trying to recover, the one thing everyone I have spoken to agreed was the hardest challenge, was the personal toll it took. When we were stripped of being able to see our loved ones, to hug them, hold them close, or to give them a kiss we felt it keenly. When we were unable to shake someone's hand and couldn't go to the pub, restaurant or sporting event, we really missed that social interaction. Everything moved online and I for one was immensely grateful for my family, friends and business colleagues who I could still interact with on some level. That was what got me through, yet, had I been more single-minded during my business years, perhaps I wouldn't have had so many wonderful people to lean on when the chips were down. Money was no leveller to the pandemic. Rich or poor, we all endured the same. The only difference was in how many of us were able to support each other through business (and personal) networks.

A commitment I made when I sold my last business in 2016 was to pass on the knowledge and experience I had built up which continues to be my mission. Learning the lesson about single-mindedness is just one nugget of wisdom I'd like to impart. Sure, as I've said, we need to be focused on our goals and sometimes we might need to prioritise our businesses, but trust me when I say that we should never lose sight of what is really important.

What good are riches if there is no one mourning your loss? As with everything in business, it's about balance and considering how single-minded your attitude is can make a huge difference to that balance.

Be focused when you need to be focused. Be present when you need to be present.

Keep your dreams alive.

Keep believing in yourself.

And keep believing in that great piece of advice I was given (on the opposite page). You won't regret it.

~ ~ ~ ~

~ 26 ~

EMBRACE LIFE'S EXPERIENCES ~ THEY SHAPE US

"The value of experience is not in seeing much, but in seeing wisely."
~ William Osler

When I was growing up, I remember being told on many occasions, not to spend time with one friend or another because they were a 'bad influence'. I'm sure you can relate.

It was our parents' role to keep us safe and provide us with the wisdom they felt we needed in order to go out into the big wide world. They would watch from the sidelines as dubious friends tried to mould us to their (bad) way of thinking and then gently (or not so gently!) encourage us to make different choices. They knew that we would be influenced by those around us, yet, as adults, we seem to forget this and are often guilty of surrounding ourselves by those who have a negative impact on our lives.

Conversely, if we surround ourselves with positive influences, perhaps those who have achieved the level of success we seek (however you choose to define success), there is a large chance their positive influence will rub off on us.

I was once advised to split those with whom I associated into three groups:

1. Those I spent too much time with and were, in reality, a constant drain on my life. Anyone who fell into this category was to be removed from my life or, at the very least, their time spent with me was to be severely limited. Otherwise I would be at risk of becoming a constant drain on others in exactly the same way.

2. Those I didn't spend enough time with who were constantly building me up and telling me they believed in me. They were enabling me to succeed (perhaps without me realising it) and I was advised to spend more time with those in this group.

3. Those whose company I enjoyed, but didn't see fitting into my future life. People who I very much liked, but who weren't assisting my growth. These I was to reduce the amount of time I spent with them.

I know this might sound harsh but after a couple of years doing this, I found myself almost pre-selecting those who provided with the most beneficial environment. To be clear, this is not being selfish. We all know how it feels to be drained by someone who wants more of you than you are willing or able to give. In the long run it does neither you nor them any favours, yet there will be someone out there who is a perfect connection for them. It's just not you - and that's okay.

Maybe we need to heed our parents early advice when it comes to those we allow to influence us. It takes discipline, but in my experience, surrounding myself with like-minded individuals has created nothing but positivity. Which is far better than living a negative existence.

One area this can be tricky, though, is when we are working in a job we don't enjoy and it is getting us down. It's so easy to be dragged lower and lower in this situation, but I always suggest to those I work with, that they try to find the positives and keep those front of mind.

Every person, every job, every experience we encounter throughout our lives will teach us something that will lead us somewhere else. That's the beauty of how our lives are intricately connected. If though, you are in a situation that is draining you, try to find the lessons within. Try to work out what you can take from it that will help you move forward once a more appropriate opportunity comes along. For example:

- If you are on the phone regularly (in a job you dislike), try celebrating the fact that you are building relationships and learning how to communicate more effectively.
- If you are struggling in a face to face environment, remember that this is helping you to understand a customer's needs and how best to deal with these.
- Look at how every experience will directly benefit you in the future, rather than hating every moment and declaring it all a complete waste of time.

People buy people. They always have done and they always will.

We don't buy companies. We buy people.

Take the positives from every experience and every relationship, and use these to help you grow

~ ~ ~ ~

HAVE YOU EVER SAID, 'IT'S NOT FAIR!'?

"Life is never fair and perhaps it is a good thing for most of us that it is not."
~ Oscar Wilde

Business and life sometimes isn't fair.

Do you ever feel that you are constantly peddling uphill or your business appears to be going backwards?

Running a business can be very complex with its fair share of ups and downs. Hopefully there will be more ups than downs, but it's not uncommon to feel like it's always the other way around.

If you are a sole trader, business can be a lonely place and if you have no one to speak to, no one to turn to or share the burdens with then that feeling of loneliness is exacerbated. This is often the time we become the most vulnerable and can start to believe that life is incredibly unfair.

The key, when it comes to business, lies in planning. If we are able to plan, then we will be much more prepared for the bad days. However, planning or working on your business can be difficult. As business owners, particularly solo business owners, we can get bogged down in the day to day 'doing' of our business and find it hard to take a step back and find the time to work 'on' the business.

When you started your own business, I bet you were excited to be doing something for yourself. Freedom beckoned! And then you realised that as well as doing what you are good at (i.e.. what the business was set up to do), you also have to do **everything** else. The accounts, the buying and selling, the contracts, the legal and HR bits, the website, the marketing, the online solutions, answering the phone, making the tea ... and it wasn't long before that initial excitement turned to dread, fear and worry.
When you get to this stage, you don't know what to do. It is very difficult to be positive when you are surrounded by so much negativity. This is when life really does not seem to be fair.

I set up my Advertising Agency in 1987 with a colleague who was my business partner until 2007. Just over a year after he left the business, I went through the toughest time of my life in what I can only describe as a depression – a recession that hit so many businesses that many went under. For those businesses that survived (thankfully mine included), it took 4 or 5 years of treading water to come out the other side.

It was hard going and life felt unfair at times, however because I had taken the time to plan for these eventualities, the business was able to (eventually) weather the storm. Planning, as I talk about in other articles, is ongoing, yet what kick-started this for me was the personal development programme I participated in way back when I started out. This gave me the attitude and skills I have needed to enjoy the good and navigate the bad - which is what all business owners should do.

If you don't know where to start, try searching for online courses about business planning or personal development, or read some of the books I recommend at the end.

Life is never fair, as Oscar Wilde said, so if we can accept that and figure out a way to turn the tide a little more in our favour, we'll handle the unfairness a good deal better than our competitors.

~ ~ ~ ~

~ 28 ~

JUST WORKING HARD ~ IS IT ENOUGH?

"The past cannot be changed. The future is yet in your power."
~ Unknown

The inspiration for this article came from a video I watched by one of the top business coaches in the USA.

"We can never think we know everything, as that is the time we start going backwards."
~ Darren Hardy

The video I watched was about 'The Four Horsemen of the Apocalypse' and how Conquest, War, Hunger and Death related to business. It was packed with good information to help the small business community survive and thrive in the most testing time (i.e. COVID-19 era) many of us will have gone through. However, the advice only works if you **take action** and you **take it now**.

Technology is part of our everyday lives but I really do fear for businesses who use it too much, as I firmly believe they are walking on very thin ice. Large tech companies like Amazon, Google, Apple and Facebook are a massive risk to our businesses and our lives. These four companies and many others like them are eroding the business communities before our eyes without us even noticing, and we do need to wake up. Unless you've seen this video, it's unlikely you've realised that this is happening. I recommend giving it a watch and I also recommend you take some time to consider how much of your business is and depends on, being online.

In my opinion it is *vital* that when we are marketing our business, we *don't do everything online*. We *have to have an offline presence,* too, however we also have to understand what to do with that offline presence.

Because so much is changing so quickly, we need to make sure we future proof our income. As the quote said, the future is in our power and in our hands. The COVID-19 pandemic and its lasting effects should have shown us what can happen if we don't protect our income. Too many people and businesses live for the now and don't have money put aside for a rainy day.

We cannot assume there will never be another pandemic or global event; in all likelihood there will be, even if it's a relatively short-term recession. Yet how many of us have improved our planning since the pandemic? How many businesses have a slush fund available? Sadly, far too few.

Businesses without plans, savings, structures, systems, processes and little to no foundation can literally fall at any time. Whilst there will undoubtedly be 'external' influencing factors, when everything is stripped back, they are the true architects of their downfall by not adapting and changing to the circumstances, market, competition, technology and environment around them.

Most business owners are working hard. In fact many are working too hard, but the problem is they are getting nowhere. Many seem to relish and brag about the fact they work 80 or 90 hours a week which, as far as I am concerned, is nothing to brag about. All this says to me is that you are not working smart.

Working hard alone will never allow us to reach true success, we have to work smart, too. We *have to spend quality time* working on our business - every week.

We need to be ahead of the game. We need to see what is happening around us. We need to follow trends and we must put ourselves in a position so that whatever comes along, we can still operate our business.

The future *is* in our power, but *only if we learn from the past*.

Use both online and offline resources to market your business and to really get ahead, use professional help and support.

Remember: to run a business effectively, you cannot do everything yourself.

~ ~ ~ ~

~ 29 ~

TAKING RESPONSIBILITY IN EVERYTHING YOU DO

"The moment you take responsibility for everything in your life is the moment you can change anything in your life."
~ Hal Elrod

In my opinion, the quote by Hal Elrod is spot on. In order to achieve anything, we have to take responsibility for everything in our lives. Not just in business. I thought, therefore, that it might be helpful to summarise some areas where we all need to be responsible.

Relationships with our spouse or life partner - I have been married to the same wonderful woman since 1981. In my younger years I didn't always take responsibility for how I handled our relationship, but thankfully, I learned how important it was to work on this. Now, I take responsibility for everything I do and work out how I can make things better. Relationships need work - constantly, but we can only do this work if we appreciate our individual responsibilities within (the relationship).

Relationships with our children - We all have to accept responsibility for our children. How they become as grown ups has everything to do with how they were brought up - in my opinion. The responsibility we take for giving them the best start directly translates to how they move on in their own lives and take on their own parental roles. Of course there are always going to be grey areas around the nature vs nurture debate, however that does not affect the responsibilities we have as parents.

Responsibility to our business - We are entirely responsible for where our business is today. We cannot blame external circumstances. We have to take full responsibility for the business we have created and the position we are in right now. I know there are those who disagree, and of course, there are going to be external influences, but ultimately we must take responsibility for our planning (or lack thereof) to combat these external influences.

Responsibility to our staff - If we employ staff, we are totally responsible for their Health and Safety whilst in our offices and on company time. Though there might legitimately be some accountability on a member of staff for a particular incident, the way of the world now is such that everything lands squarely on the employer's shoulders. One way to keep everyone happy, safe and on board with their own areas of responsibility is to learn to be a great leader and team player. Being a boss is not about dictatorship.

Responsibility to clients - Would you rather have a business where you are constantly looking for new clients or one where clients come back time and time again? A well-functioning business should welcome both new and return custom, however if we don't take responsibility and learn from our mistakes - or even just admit to them! - then we are unlikely to maintain good business relationships. Take responsibility and don't be afraid to admit to being wrong. Looking after our clients and existing relationships is paramount to building a successful, long-lasting business.

Responsibility to others - How we handle our personal responsibility will impact the safety of others. In some cases, it can potentially save lives. If we think about the COVID-19 pandemic, every single one of us had to 'up' our personal responsibility for the good of not only ourselves, but everyone we connected with. Some, sadly, failed to take adequate responsibility during this time, which has had long-term repercussions on our services and economy. If you are in a position of leadership, act like a leader. People are looking to you for direction. Be strong, have strong convictions. You may not be right all the time, and if you are wrong admit it. Take responsibility. Do what is right for the greater cause and not for what benefits you the most.

By acting responsibly - which is all we can do as *individuals* - we are going to benefit *everyone*.

We ALL need to take personal responsibility for everything we do, and it is only when we do this we can truly change our lives and the lives of those around us.

Be responsible in all that you do.

Look at the greater cause.

Do what is right.

Think of others - and we all win.

~ ~ ~ ~

~ 30 ~

THEORY OR EXPERIENCE?

"The only source of knowledge is experience." ~ *Albert Einstein*

Now before I get into this article, I want to clarify that I am not saying *theories* are irrelevant; *theories* are often where greatness begins. *Combining theory and experience* though, in my opinion, is the absolute holy grail.

Undoubtedly, we learn from experience and any experience - whether good or bad - adds value to our offering. Simply put, good experiences will tell us what we are doing well and what we should continue to do and bad experiences will tell us the opposite. It is in from these bad experiences that the most important of lessons can be learned - as long as we are smart enough not to repeat the behaviour that led to the bad experience!

When we are working with clients, our experiences add immense value to how we can help them. I love to know what people do for a living, how they help their clients, and how they got from where they were to where they currently are. I remember being at a networking event many years ago and other than the host who was there early, there was only one other person and myself there at that time. After we had introduced ourselves, I asked him what he did for a living. He told me he was a business coach. I asked him how long he had been doing it, and he told me it was his first week. I asked him what he did last week and he said he was in IT. You can probably imagine what I was thinking.

Of course, we all need to start somewhere, but he had no experience as a business coach, no training as such, and was actively networking for clients. Whilst he may have done a crash course on the theories, I would have been sceptical of outsourcing to him, purely because he didn't have that second ingredient of experience.

It's a tough one, though. How do we get experience if no one is prepared to give us a chance?

- If you are due to have major surgery, how much more confident would you be of a positive outcome if you knew that your surgeon had successfully carried out the same procedure many times? Or would you be okay if they had simply read 'Brain Surgery 101'?

- Or maybe you're learning to drive with an instructor who has only just passed their test, or worse, only passed the theory part. How safe would you feel then?

We are all going to feel more confident if the person we are working with (outsourcing to) has ample experience. That's just human nature.

If we, as business owners are looking for partners or support in certain areas of our business it is, in my opinion, critical to check the credentials of anyone we are considering - before they start work.

As we've covered in many of the previous articles, outsourcing is the key to running a successful business, but only if we make sure to do our research and find the right people to outsource to - those who have both experience and theoretical knowledge.

If you're concerned that hiring a professional is expensive, try hiring an amateur - it will cost you ten times as much.

That being said, as I eluded to a few paragraphs ago, we all need to start somewhere and there is a place for 'newbies'. What we need to ensure is if we are going to give them the opportunity to gain experience (which in my opinion we absolutely should), then we need to give them not only the theoretical tools that they need, but the help and support of others around them who can impart their experience and wisdom.

As I said:

THEORY + EXPERIENCE = THE BUSINESS HOLY GRAIL

~ ~ ~ ~

~ 31 ~

WE HAVE TO LIVE WITH THE CHOICES WE MAKE

"Everything in your life is a reflection of a choice you have made. If you want a different result, make a different choice."
~ Unknown

Someone once said to me:

"We are today in life exactly where we choose to be."

I always thought that was a bit blunt, but on reflection, it's spot on. *The choices we have made have led us to where we are today.*

We are so incredibly fortunate to live in a society where we have the freedom of choice, but with choice comes consequences and we have to be prepared to not only accept those consequences, but to live with them, too.

How, though, do we know if we are making the right or wrong decision? If the consequences or outcome are the best for us?

In truth, we don't.

Business owners across the board faced some incredibly tough decisions in the light of the COVID-19 pandemic. In the UK, we were given certain guidelines but when those were lifted, it was up to us to consider how we were going to move forward. Did pubs, for example, open their doors again and act as if nothing had happened? Did shops agree to only serve people who continued to wear masks? Did office workers remain working from home, just in case?

In hindsight we can see that no one had the answers and no decision was wrong or right. Each business, regardless of structure or sector, had to make the decision they felt was best for them at the time - and then live with the consequences.

Therefore, if a shop refused to sell to anyone not wearing a mask, for example, they needed to understand that customers who didn't want to wear masks would go elsewhere.

And that this would negatively impact their bottom line.

If a pub threw open its doors without restriction, then chances are they would see a huge upturn in business - especially after two lockdowns when everyone just wants to get out and feel 'normal' again. On the face of it, the outcome of this decision would be positive, but there is a responsibility for them to also consider potential negative impacts to this decision.

The point is, every decision we make has a consequence and some consequences may be long-lasting.

The good news is that from a business perspective, there is a middle ground. There is a place where we can make both short-term and long-term decisions. Perhaps, in the case of the pub, we do 'staged' openings. Maybe a few tables at a time. Adding more as the weeks go on. Short-term we are open for business again, long-term we are being responsible.

Any business MUST HAVE a long term plan and vision that can be fluid and flexible. It must also be relatable to those around us and easy to understand. The last thing we want to do is alienate staff, clients or potential new customers.

With a long-term plan and vision, we can factor in as many potential consequences as we can foresee. We can also ask other business owners with more experience for their comments on our plans. We will almost certainly have forgotten one or other eventuality and we cannot accurately plan for something like a pandemic because there are too many unknowns BUT, if we really consider the decisions we need to make and work through the potential consequences, we will be in a much more robust position to cope when times are toughest.

We cannot and should not make decisions that impact the future of our businesses on our own - especially if we are going into unchartered waters.

We need to reach out to mentors, those who have been where we have.

Whilst we are still gaining our own experience and learning how to make our own decisions, we can lean on these mentors - there is no one better placed to offer support.

Then, even though we're still going to make mistakes, we can choose our decisions more wisely and be more prepared for their outcomes - whether they are good or bad.

~ ~ ~ ~

~ 32 ~

WHAT IS YOUR WHY?

"All of our dreams can come true, if we have the courage to pursue them." ~
Walt Disney

Why did you get into business in the first place?

Probably for most – if not all of us – its because we had a **dream.** We don't use this term as much in the UK as in countries such as the USA, but a *'dream'* is essentially the same as our *'why'* when it comes to business, so I'm going to use the term *'why'* here, for simplicity.

What is your *why*? I'm sure, as a business owner, you've been asked this countless times because, let's face it, everything we do within our business is driven by our *why*. However, what if we don't have a *why* or are unclear on it? Or perhaps our *why* isn't big enough. Making a statement along the lines of, *'I do what I do to support my family and put food on the table'* is not a big enough *why*. If that is your only *why*, you could work for someone else and do a totally different job. You don't need the added pressure of being your own boss.

Let me ask you a question: If time and money were not an issue and you could do anything you wanted to do in life, what would you do?

Think about it and think about it hard. The answer to this, is your **'passion'.**

Then think about why you want to do this particular thing. What is it about your passion that makes you enjoy it so much? The answer to this, is your **'why'.**

If what you are doing to generate income is your passion, it will never feel like a job.

Most of us just 'end up' in the business or job we are in. Often it wasn't planned, circumstances just led us in that direction. If we are not happy in this business or job and are just going through the motions, then we are more than likely 'stuck in a rut'.

I like to think of this as the treadmill of life. We have walked a certain way for a certain time and have become stuck in that place. Then, we get to an age where we excuse feeling unfulfilled because we are 'too old to do anything else'. So we continue walking that same treadmill until we retire. Not a great way to live, eh!

If your *passion/why/dream* is big enough, the facts don't count:

- Legend has it that Walt Disney was turned down 302 times before finally achieving financing for his dream of creating Walt Disney World.
- It's also been said that KFC founder Colonel Sanders was rejected 1009 times before finding a taker for his chicken recipe.
- J K Rowling's manuscript for Harry Potter was rejected 12 times before it was published.

There are countless other examples, like these. How easy would it be for them to have given up on their dream?

If you have lost your dream or why, then perhaps it's time to revisit this. Maybe you need to discover a *new* dream or why. Without that passion to drive you then it will always be harder to keep going and you will never be able to run on the treadmill of life, or even get off it altogether!

If it helps, do a bit of research about others who have maintained belief in their dream/passion/why - and I'm not just talking about famous people. Ask those around you what their passion is. What their why is. What their dream is.

Some will have achieved it. Some will be on the journey towards it. Others will be on a completely different path.

Everyone's business and life path is unique but with *passion* and a solid *why*, you will be able to achieve your *dream*.

~ ~ ~ ~

~ 33 ~

WHAT MAKES US WHO WE ARE?

"It is not enough to have the courage of your convictions, you must also have the courage to have your convictions challenged."
~ Christopher Phillips

I know I am not everyone's cup of tea. I know I have the potential to piss people off at times - never intentionally - but I have always had courage of my convictions. Moreover, I've always understood that they will be challenged and I am okay with that. I will stand firm in my beliefs - beliefs I am convinced were moulded from an early age.

Here is a potted history of me, and why I am certain this is the case:

I was born August 27, 1957. My sister Julie came along 3 years later on the 20 February 1960. Julie was born with dislocated hips - not a major problem today but it was in 1960. The first 7 years of her life were spent in and out of the Royal National Orthopaedic hospital in Stanmore which was 20 miles from where we lived. My parents and I made that journey 3 times a week at least, meaning that up until I was 10, life pretty much revolved around Julie.

Now I am not complaining. This is exactly the way it should have been and I was rewarded with a new dinky toy car every now and again. At that age I knew no different, but as you can imagine, when my sister came home, my parents wrapped her in cotton wool - a protection they extended to me. As a result I was quite a shy kid but I was always polite and courteous. I was never in trouble but struggled with exams though I did manage to pass the 11+ and get into grammar school. Though I was reserved, I made friends okay and when I left school at 16, I started work in a bank because mum told me it was a good secure job.

As I've mentioned in other articles, I was expected to study for additional exams within the bank in order to progress, and I really wasn't up for that so I left and began working in airfreight which was an industry both my sister and mum worked in. It was during this period that I met my wife, Denise.

When we were looking for a house to buy, mum was insistent we remained close. We settled on a property about 20 miles away in the end. I loved my parents but we wanted to forge our own way in life, and did not want them just popping round when they felt like it.

A few months after we were married, Denise and I were introduced to Network Marketing by a neighbour. We went along to a presentation which changed our life. Through this and Denise's belief in me, I knew I would be in a position to start my own company before the age of 30.

That's not to say I knew what I was going to do because I didn't. But through the educational support programme element of Network Marketing, my thinking and attitude changed, allowing me to believe that anything was possible. We were hanging around successful and success minded people, and their attitude, inspiration, and motivation rubbed off on me in abundance.

I started my own business on the 3rd of September 1987, one week after my 30th birthday. My dad told me I had lost the plot and was being irresponsible packing up a job with a regular salary for a business with no guarantees, especially with a baby on the way.

Twelve months later I nearly proved him right. The business was £24000 in debt at the end of that first year. At that point my business partner and I realised we hadn't been taking it seriously enough and that we needed to run it like a 'proper business'. With renewed energy and unwavering belief in what we were doing, we turned it around. I went on to run this business for 33yrs. How? And what kept me going?

- I always looked for opportunities.
- I always asked questions.
- I NEVER just accepted what anyone told me as gospel.
- I checked everything out.
- Once I had made a decision I had unshakeable belief.
- I regularly reviewed my beliefs.
-

As you can imagine there is not much I haven't been through in the last 40 years. I have been close to going out of business twice and I know the strength of my beliefs aren't always appreciated but I follow my gut. I don't believe in following the herd. My advice?

- Develop the strength of a lion with decisions made from the heart.
- Accept we are not all the same
- We are all free to make the decisions we choose and choose our beliefs.

Do you have courage in yours?

~ ~ ~ ~

~ 34 ~

WHAT MAKES US STAND OUT FROM THE CROWD?

"They laugh at me because I am different. I laugh at them because they are all the same." ~ Kurt Cobain

I have a great friend and business colleague, Phil Strachan, who always talks about the importance of businesses standing out from the crowd and not being just A N Other. When I came across the Kurt Cobain quote, I decided that I wanted to put my own slant on both this and Phil's excellent advice.

Here's what I know about me:
- I have never followed anyone else's agenda.
- I hated working for someone else.
- I would have been crap in the Army as I hate taking orders.
- I am surprised I lasted 14 years as an employee.

Here's what I know about small business owners:
- We need to be different.
- We need to operate differently.
- We need to act differently.
- No one teaches us how to run a business.
- When we leave an 'employed' role and become 'self-employed', we still have the mentality of an 'employee'.
- We cannot run a business if we still think of ourselves as 'employees'.

Here's what I did and what you need to do:
1. Work on our own personal development - we all need continuing education.
2. Go networking - this is an art, so you need to learn how to maximise the opportunity.
3. Learn how to outsource and who to outsource to - check credentials of those you outsource to.
4. Look at outsourcing as an investment and not a cost.
5. Spend time working ON your business - at least 10% of every week.
6. Get a mentor or a coach to help you build a better business - but check their credentials first.

Remember:

- Owning a business is a honour.
- It should be part of us.
- It should mirror who we are as a person.
- We should run it with strong values.
- We should run it the right way.
- We should do the right thing for our clients.

My family never really understood why I left secure employment to set up on my own. Dad thought I had lost the plot. Though, those closest were not necessarily laughing at me, they were not entirely supportive either.

Entrepreneurs are different, we don't follow the crowd which is why we need to make sure that our businesses are different, too. We don't want to be just A N Other, we want to be the one that stands out from the crowd.

Being different is good, it's exciting, it's an adventure. It's stressful at times, but being and doing something different will never be easy.

This is what makes success such a precious thing.

~ ~ ~ ~

~ 35 ~

YOU ARE THE PROBLEM TO YOUR PROBLEMS

"The way we see the problem is the problem."
~ Stephen Covey

Choices

- You are totally responsible for where you are in life today.
- You have choices - every day of your life.
- The choices you made in the past lead you to where you are today.
- Where you will be tomorrow will be down to the choices you make today.
- Choose wisely.

Problems

- You create your own problems.
- You cannot blame the problems you have on someone or something else.
- You are the problem to your problems.
- The sooner you understand that, the sooner you will start moving forward.
- Too many people are too quick to blame external situations for where they are in life.

Opportunities

- Instead of looking at the problem, look at the opportunity the problem creates.
- If you keep looking at the problem, you will only ever see more problems.
- If you look at possibilities, you will see opportunities.
- If you *don't want problems*, then *do nothing*.
- The more you strive for success, the more problems you will have.
- Welcome these problems as opportunities to learn. Do not run from them.
- When you look for opportunities, you will see more opportunities.
- As one door opens so there will be another ten doors behind that door. Just open the door.

Attitude

- Your problem is not the problem, its your attitude about the problem.
- If your mind is not right and you focus on negatives, you will never see the opportunities.
- A healthy positive mind will always help you to build a better, more secure business.

Awareness

- Failure to spot opportunities in your business could have serious future repercussions.
- Be aware of opportunities.
- Act upon them to make sure you stay ahead of your competitors.
- Businesses who don't spot opportunities are more likely to fail.
- Businesses who don't act on opportunities are more likely to fail.
- Businesses who fail almost always blame this failure on external factors.
- The businesses failure is almost always due to a lack of awareness.

Remember:

1. Positive mindset.
2. Wise choices.
3. Personal acceptance.
4. Look for opportunities.
5. Start planning for next year. Now. It's never too early.

Don't be the problem to your problems.

~ ~ ~ ~

~ 36 ~

YOU ARE WHAT YOU DO ~ ACTION!

"Action is the foundational key to all success."
~ Pablo Picasso

"When your action contradicts your words, your words don't mean anything"

We all know that nothing happens without action yet we all know someone - and it could be ourselves - who has never done what they said they were going to do. They will blame anything/anyone but themselves for their lack of action or success.

A quote I heard many years ago from a very highly respected and successful business friend was:

"To know and not to do is not to know."

Education shouldn't only be for a thirst of knowledge, it should also be used to inspire action. **Actions prove who someone is, words just prove who they want to be.**

We never know what the results are going to be from our actions, but it's pretty easy to figure out what our results will be *without* action. We need clearly defined goals to help us take action which in turn keeps us on track towards our goals. **We must take action based on where we want to be and not where we currently are.**

Positive actions combined with positive beliefs will produce positive results. Reputation is built on what *actions we take* and *not on those we say we* are going to take. When our actions match our words, this builds trust and respect therefore we need to do what we say we will do - at all times.

Taking action can also help us to overcome our fears. They will move us out of our comfort zone which is where we need to be in order for the magic to happen. **If we don't know what to do, often we will do nothing which means nothing changes.**

Whilst going to seminars and reading personal development books is a great start and helps to build a solid and durable business foundation, doing *this alone will not achieve anything*. We still have to put the action in. **Education is vital but useless without action.**

Taking action doesn't necessarily take money or experience. All it takes is a willingness and a desire to do something different with the aim of facilitating change. *Not taking action will almost certainly have a detrimental effect on your mental health.*

I promise:

- Taking action will stop you complaining.
- No one complains when they are taking action; they are too busy being busy in the "Action zone".
- Taking action will also help you develop new skills,

Remember:

- Action is not always related to business.
- Our actions towards family and friends and to clients and suppliers speak volumes about us.
- A hug can sometimes say so much more than words.
- Your actions when someone has a differing opinion determines the person you are.

How do you act?

Make sure your actions are louder than your words. That way no one can be in any doubt as to the kind of person you are.

> *"Vision without action is merely a dream, Action without vision just passes the time. Vision with action can change the world."*
> *~ Joel Arthur Barker*

~ ~ ~ ~

3 Section Three

(Business) Self-Development

37.   BEWARE OF IDIOTS WRAPPED IN TIN FOIL

38.   STOP PULLING YOURSELF IN ALL DIRECTIONS

39.   DO YOU ASK WHY?

40.   DISCIPLINE ~ GOAL SETTING VS GOAL ACHIEVING

41.   ARE YOU A CONFORMIST?

42.   ARE YOU ON THE RIGHT PATH?

43.   ASK FOR HELP

44.   COMFORT ZONE

45.   BIG BOY/GIRL PANTS TIME EVERYONE!

46.   DO YOU CREATE GOOD HABITS?

47.   DO YOU FEEL LIKE YOU ARE GOING UP THE DOWN ESCALATOR?

48.   DO YOU MAKE EXCUSES?

49.   HOW DO NEGATIVE SITUATIONS AFFECT YOUR ATTITUDE?

50.   HOW DO YOU COPE WITH SETBACKS?

51.   HOW GOOD ARE YOU AT ADAPTING?

52.   HOW STRONG ARE YOUR COMMITMENTS?

53.   OPTIMIST OR PESSIMIST?

54.   PERSONAL DEVELOPMENT

55.   TRUST ~ YEARS TO BUILD, SECONDS TO BREAK, YEARS TO REPAIR

56.   WHAT DO WE SAY WHEN WE TALK TO OURSELVES?

57.   YOU ARE NOT GOING TO GET OUT OF LIFE ALIVE

58.   ARE YOU BORN TO STAND OUT, NOT JUST FIT IN?

BEWARE OF IDIOTS WRAPPED IN TIN FOIL

"Sometimes your knight in shining armour turns out to be an idiot wrapped in tin foil."
~ Unknown

I originally wrote this article as we were in the midst of the worldwide COVID-19 pandemic. The world had pretty much ground to a halt and business owners - myself included - were being forced to review our business and practices. For some it provided the opportunity to pivot or shift direction, others were able to discover new income streams or more innovate ways of working. I remember being hugely encouraged by how many businesses evolved to support our essential services here in the UK, which reminded me of an old quote:

"Every adversity, every failure, every heartache, carries with it the seed of an equal or greater benefit " ~ Napoleon Hill

When we take time to look carefully at our businesses, we will almost certainly see opportunities that we would not have noticed before. These opportunities will have been under our noses, but because we *'always do what we have always done',* we don't notice them.

As business owners we should always be evolving:

"If you always do what you've always done, you'll always get what you've always got " ~ Henry Ford

"The definition of insanity is doing the same thing over and over and expecting different results " ~ Rita Mae Brown

(NB. You might see this quote attributed to Albert Einstein, however none of his works ever contained these lines. The quote originates from a novel, 'Sudden Death', written by Rita Mae Brown in 1983.)

It is my opinion and belief that we must always be creative and spend quality time working on our businesses.

One challenge I come across often, is business owners who are trying to improve their productivity or efficiency, however, that will never happen if they continue to work alone. Here's my list of top tips to help your business move towards increased productivity and efficiency:

1. Stop trying to do everything yourself.
2. You cannot be all things to all people.
3. Focus on what you are good at and do it well and outsource everything else to those more qualified than you. Yes it will cost you money but you have to look at it as an investment in your business and not a cost. This will allow you more time to focus on what you are good at.
4. Do not employ anyone without the help of an HR professional.
5. Don't spend one full day a week doing your books when a qualified book-keeper will do it in a few hours and do it properly.
6. Make sure you employ the services of a coach or mentor.
7. Make sure your message is right and you are in the right place to target your audience.

In summary, if we focus on what we are good at and outsource everything else, we will make our businesses a lot more efficient, productive and professional.

When outsourcing, always check the credentials of your potential supplier/partner. Check their linked in profile. Ask some of those who have given great testimonials how easy it was to work with that supplier. Check with some of their other clients, too if you can.

Also, though it may seem obvious, it's good practice to look at more than one supplier/partner before making your choice. Every business operates differently with different personalities and internal dynamics. Even though each supplier can in theory, offer you the same outcome, you might find yourself more in tune with one than another which will lead to an improved and more beneficial working relationship. Try not to focus on cost too much at this stage. Use this as a fact-finding mission and ask lots of questions. If it turns out that the most expensive is going to be the best fit, then I would recommend doing a cost-benefit analysis to work out if this supplier is going to be viable.

Don't rush into taking someone on, and certainly don't take someone on that you meet for the first time. There are some excellent salespeople out there who literally could sell ice to the Eskimos, however, that doesn't necessarily make them good at what they do.

Knights wore armour for a reason. Don't protect your business with tin foil.

~ ~ ~ ~

~ 38 ~

STOP PULLING YOURSELF IN ALL DIRECTIONS

"I feel like I'm being pulled in a hundred different directions and my feet are stuck in cement."
~ Elizabeth Acevedo

One of the most important lessons we need to learn as business owners is that we can't be all things to all people. We **have** to stop pulling ourselves in all directions. As well as being damaging to our businesses, it can also be damaging to our health and relationships.

The fact is: we are all gifted with 24 hours in a day. None of us get any more or any less. It is how we manage and use those hours that makes the difference.

Priorities will vary but in my opinion, there has to be a sensible balance. If we don't have our life in balance and we spend too many hours working in our businesses, we are damaging every other area of our lives.

- We have to sleep and eat.
- We have to spend time with our families and friends.
- We have to have a social life. If we don't have 'downtime' then we will undoubtedly burn out or find our mental health deteriorating.
- We have to spend time running our businesses ... *but not at the expense of other areas of our lives.*

Most small business owners work more hours than they ever did working for someone else, and probably earn less money – but generally they have no desire to return to working for someone else. ***The beauty of running our own business is the freedom it allows - however, we must give ourselves the opportunity to experience and embrace that freedom.***

I started my own business in 1987. We did not have computer, or a website or an email address. Everything was handwritten and typed. Desks had hard-wired telephones and we actually used them. It was the only way to contact our clients. The arrival of a fax machine felt otherworldly, yet now, technology has evolved so much, all that remains of those days are our fading memories. Modern technology has made it possible to do more in a day than we used to do in a week and the time flies by. Days, weeks, months, years ... I was constantly saying to my employees that we 'go to work on a Monday morning and by the time we go home at the end of the day, it's Friday.' Because that's how it feels. However, that doesn't mean it's good.

Yes, we can do more, but we're working more hours than ever and given that we still only have the same 24 hours in the day that we had in 1987, some part of our lives are being sacrificed.

From the time I set up the business in 1987 through to when I sold and exited in 2020, I never worked more than 50 hours a week. I needed to maintain a balance for my own health and well-being as well as for my family, but I also learned very early on to know what I was good at and what I was not so good at.

I emphasise this throughout these articles, but it is the *biggest key to running a successful business and maintaining a good life*. **Please: ASK FOR HELP**.

The sooner you understand you have to ask for help, the sooner everything in your life will begin to look better. If you don't know who to ask for help, try reaching out to your network on LinkedIn or other social media, or attending a networking event. Once you begin to surround yourself with others in a similar situation, solutions will present themselves.

Try making your next business year THE year for spearheading countless successful crusades. Make it a year for running your business better than you have ever run it before, and above all ...

...make sure you know when to ask for help.

~ ~ ~ ~

~ 39 ~

DO YOU ASK WHY?

"All highly competent people continually search for ways to keep learning, growing and improving. They do that by asking WHY. After all, the person who knows HOW will always have a job, but the person who knows WHY will always be the boss."
~ Benjamin Franklin

How often do you ask WHY?

Do you question the WHY behind what you are told or just accept it?

WHY **would** we question things?

WHY **wouldn't** we question things?

I always remember someone telling me that WHY is the most powerful question in the English language. Children ask it all the time. This is how they learn. Parents, on the other hand, who get understandably frustrated by the never-ending WHY, often get to the stage where they respond with 'because it is' or 'because I said so.' To a child, this is a far from satisfactory answer but to the parent, well, they've simply run out of good enough replies.
Even if the child finds this answer unsatisfactory, they are forced to accept it because there is no alternative.

As adults, we often accept everything we are told, perhaps because we learned to as children, but also because we see everyone else doing the same thing. If we are all doing the same thing, there is no need to question WHY.

IT JUST IS. (Ring any bells?).

I was once asked what drove me to run the same business for over 30 years. My reply was that I kept the business and myself fresh by asking questions. It kept me on my toes and ahead of my competitors. Instead of accepting, I questioned everything I was told.

I realised that knowing HOW to do something was one thing, but I wanted to know WHY. As the quote from Benjamin Franklin says, the person who asks

WHY will be the boss of the person who knows how.

There are countless studies and statistical analyses of conformity - why we conform and who of us are most likely to conform - but the average suggestion is that around 75-80% people will conform to the 'norm'. Regardless of the merits of that 'norm'. Of that percentage, a staggering high proportion don't even question why they are conforming.

THEY JUST DO. (Sound familiar?)

It follows then, that if majority conform, only a small minority continue to question, and it this minority in my experience, who are running successful businesses or 'winning' at life.

The best way to get context in any situation is to ask WHY. A lot. Asking WHY eliminates confusion caused by preconceived assumptions. Preconceived assumptions are fuelled by lack of knowledge or (at best) partial knowledge so by asking WHY we can define a clear path. Everyone will be on the same page.

> *"To err is human, to forgive divine."*
> *~ Alexander Pope (from An Essay on Criticism).*

It's human to exercise caution and to make mistakes. That doesn't mean we're failing, it means we're learning. Asking WHY is the best way to learn.

We all need to know WHY in life. WHY we are doing what we are doing, otherwise there is no purpose or direction. If we don't know where we are going or WHY we are going there, we are probably not going to like where we end up.

During a recent podcast interview I was asked to give one 'top tip'. I replied that we should ask WHY - and ask it constantly.

Before you do anything in life or are asked to do anything, ask WHY?

And just don't take the standard answer, check it out. Get the facts.

Be sure of WHY you are doing anything before you do it. Trust me. You *need* to know.

~ ~ ~ ~

~ 40 ~

DISCIPLINE ~ GOAL SETTING vs GOAL ACHIEVING

"Discipline is the bridge between goals and success."
~ Jim Rohn

"Discipline is the bridge between goals and success."

This is such a powerful message; you really need to let it sink in.

With it, you will succeed, without it you won't.

This applies to everything you are striving for.

How many times have you or someone you know, said they will achieve something by a certain date, and then not put in the commitment to get there?

The only way to achieve what we want to achieve, is by putting in the hard commitment yards - which is purely down to discipline (as long as the goal is reachable).

There is a massive difference between setting goals and achieving them. Setting is easy. Setting is just words. Achieving requires total discipline - NO EXCUSES.

That being said, there are many who don't understand the intricacies of *goal setting*. In most cases, we will set ourselves a *long-term goal* and focus all of our attention on that, but the key to successful goal setting (and achieving) is in the *short term goals*. The baby steps that will cumulatively allow us to reach the long term goal.

I am a firm believer in focusing on DAILY GOALS. They are easier to *achieve* and easier to *catch up on* if you fall short on one day. If set properly, though, you should always achieve them (barring illness, injury or death!). Their achievement is reached by employing discipline.

I have written another article on Goal Setting where I talk about the discipline I needed to have when I was training for the London Marathon. Since Christmas 2020, I have decided to replicate that discipline by setting myself a daily goal to walk 10,000 steps. No excuses.

Often, I was asked what my end goal was - to which I replied that I wanted to ensure I remained fit and healthy. Setting that goal was easy, achieving it was not without its challenges.

There have been days when it has been harder to achieve than others. Days when I've had to go out either really early or later than I would like due to my workload. Occasionally I've had to clear time in my diary during the day. I found that treating it the same way I would treat a business appointment was crucial. I put it in my diary, track my steps and document my total at the end of the week.

By the end of 2021, I had completed my goal every day, and had walked just a shade under 5 millions steps with an average weekly count of 90,000 steps, and average daily count of 13,000 steps. I pushed on to reach 5 million, which I reached at the end of the 54th week - so now it was time to think about a longer term goal.

Could I do the next 5 million steps in 50 weeks, so I would have completed 10 million steps (5000 miles in 2 years) by the end of 2022. It meant adjusting my daily goal to 14,000 steps and making sure I remained disciplined, as well as catching up on days I had fallen short, for example. The last thing I wanted was to fall behind.

By the beginning of December 2022, I was almost there. In fact, I was ahead of the game and could reduce my daily count to 12,500 if I wanted. The goal of 10 million steps was achieved on the 30th December 2022 with one day to spare.

The point was, by breaking it down into daily goals, I was able to stay on top of it. The discipline at times wasn't easy, but *because I had employed short-term goals to achieve a long-term goal*, there was no way I was going to fail.

With **discipline**, you will succeed.

~ ~ ~ ~

~ 41 ~

ARE YOU A CONFORMIST?

"The opposite of courage in our society is not cowardice,
it is conformity."
~ Earl Nightingale

"Why do only 5% succeed by the time they get to retirement age? Because the rest conform, because they act like the wrong percentage group. They are in the 95% group. Why do people conform - they don't know. They believe their lives are shaped by circumstances, things that happen to them by exterior circumstances.

Why do people go to work? Why do they get up in the morning? 95% will have no idea. They do it because everyone else does it. They conform. You need to have a reason why you do what you do. Success is not purely about making money, it is doing what you want to do, not what someone else wants you to do. It's deliberately doing a predetermined job because that is what you decided to do - DELIBERATELY. Only 1 out of 20 does that. That is why there is not really any competition, and the only competition is ourselves. Those who succeed do so because they have goals. They know where they are going and they work towards their goals."

These words are from *"The Strangest Secret"* by *Earl Nightingale* and if you have never heard it, I strongly suggest you listen to it. It could have been produced in the last 12 months but it was recorded 65 years ago. Success principles never change.

It is always very easy to follow the masses. Someone once said to me many years ago, *"Observe the masses and do the opposite. The masses are always wrong"*.

When it comes to building a successful business, you cannot ever follow the masses. Remember only 1 in 20 (as above) will be successful. You need to have the courage to believe in yourself. In so many cases, **other people will believe in you long before you believe in yourself.** Surround yourself with people who believe in you.

Hanging around with successful or success minded people will have a positively profound effect on your life. I can personally vouch for this.

There will be times when you doubt the decisions you make in life - especially if they go against the 'norm' - but this is what determines those who succeed and those who don't. It takes courage to grow up and become who you really are.

Question everything. Ask WHY!

I have never been one to conform to anything. I love making MY decisions in life and not following the herd. This is one reason why I am good at what I do and why I am in a position to help as many business owners as I can. I want people to ask that question of me when I am working with clients. I certainly ask it to all my clients. I want to know *why* they do what they do.

We all need to know why we are doing what we are doing.

- Conformity will never get you the results you want - in any area of your life. Have the courage to make your own decisions, and don't do what everyone else does just because.
- Believe in yourself, and surround yourself with positive upbeat people.
- Get yourself immersed in a personal development programme.
- Have a team of people around you who are successful or success minded and if you don't believe in yourself now, you soon will.

In the words of the late, great Earl Nightingale, "Do you act like everyone else - without knowing why?"

Don't act unless you know why.

~ ~ ~ ~

~ 42 ~

DON'T BE FRIGHTENED TO ASK FOR HELP

"The only mistake you can make is not asking for help."
~ Sandeep Jauhar

From when I set up my Advertising Agency in 1987, to when I sold it almost 33yrs later, I consistently networked with other small business owners and one thing that always amazed me, was the reluctance of many to ask for help.

Most networking meetings have an abundance of people who can help small business owners including bookkeepers, HR consultants, Social Media specialists, LinkedIn support, business mentors and coaches – to name a few - and yet most small business owners try to do everything themselves.

STOP NOW!

I have said many times, we can't be all things to all people. We have to understand what we are good at and what we are not good at and then engage others to help us with the stuff we are not good at.

You cannot run a business properly without help and, whilst I appreciate you will need to pay for this help, you won't get sound business advice and support for free. When it comes to funding this help, it's about looking at the long term picture. Though it may feel like a huge initial investment, I guarantee that asking others to help you with aspects of your business will end up saving you money in the long run. Why? Because it frees you up to focus on what you are good at and what really brings the money in.

I would recommend reading *The E-Myth Revisited* by *Michael Gerber*. Reading good business books is a great habit to get into and it can be great to build up a library. That way you are also in the position to pass on those books and help support another business owner.

We can all be part of the revolution to help and support small business owners in the UK. There are currently about 4.5 million businesses that are termed as micro businesses - employ less than 10 people – and it is my belief that we should help in any way we can to ensure these businesses stay afloat.

Most people start their own business either through redundancy or because they get fed up making someone else money (!), or they may have been forced to leave an employed role for other (personal) reasons. Whilst setting up on your own is great, what most soon realise is that in addition to doing the job they once did, they now have to be a bookkeeper, a sales person, a marketing person, a social media person, a distributor ... and so on. And then, when they realise this, they also realise they can't do it all - moreover, they are not experienced enough to do it all - and this is why so many businesses fail.

Please ask for help. It will save you money in the long term. Just make sure you check the credentials of the people you get in to help and support your business.

We are all looking for a 'knight in shining armour' but if we don't properly check the credentials of those we ask for help, then beware of ending up with an 'imposter wrapped in tin foil.'

~ ~ ~ ~

~ 43 ~

YOU NEED TO GET OUT OF YOUR COMFORT ZONE

"Life begins at the end of your comfort zone."
~ Neale Donald Walsch

We can all stay rooted in our comfort zone however when we are in this place, we are often only 'going through the motions' and stop trying to stretch ourselves. If we remain 'trapped' in our comfort zone for too long, this can lead to negative thinking and emotional exhaustion, because we have nothing to challenge us.

We can get comfortable in the work environment, relationship environment or fitness environment for instance when often it is better if we stretch ourselves. Why? Because that's when we can really begin to learn and grow.

As children we were constantly moving outside of our comfort zones without realising it, but for some reason, when we reach adulthood we become stagnant, we remain in places we are comfortable and don't expand our horizons in the same way.

By way of illustration, let's assume your comfort zone is inside a circle and outside of that circle is a big wide world full of opportunities and new experiences. Most of our friends and family will be inside the circle so what can happen (if we decide to move outside of this circle) is that our loved ones will pull us back emotionally. There is safety in numbers and whilst our friends might want us to succeed and embrace new opportunities, they may also not want us to achieve more than they can. So, if a friend is stuck and unwilling to leave their own comfort zone, they might offer many reasons why we shouldn't apply for a particular promotion, for example. They recognise we have the courage to step outside of the circle and because they don't have the same courage in their lives, they are frightened of what it means for them if we do this.

Why is it so important to step outside of our comfort zone, though?

- It is important for personal growth. We constantly need to be stretching ourselves.
- When everything is comfortable, we just go through the motions. We need to be doing what is currently uncomfortable for us until it gets to a stage when it becomes comfortable. Then we look for the next area of discomfort

and work on that until that too becomes comfortable.

- Continuously moving towards the uncomfortable creates momentum and once in the rhythm, it cannot be stopped
- It will eliminate fear. We are all fearful of certain things and action and momentum will challenge those fears and move us beyond them.
- We have to programme our minds to work for us and not against us.
- Moving outside of our comfort zones is great for personal fulfilment.
- We all need to be challenged and we have total control as to how we live our lives - every day of our lives.
- Every day when we wake up we can choose to be positive or negative - and guess what? Being positive pulls opportunities and relationships towards us - being negative pushes them away.
- It will create a new source of total satisfaction.
- You will positively affect those you come in contact with.

Moving outside your comfort zone and constantly challenging yourself will have a massively powerful impact on you and all those you come in contact with.

> *"Whatever the human mind can conceive and believe, it can achieve."*
> *~ Napoleon Hill*

~ ~ ~ ~

~ 44 ~

BIG BOY/GIRL PANTS TIME!

"Put your big-boy pants on. Just adjust. You can't whine about it. You can't complain about it."
~ Kobe Bryant

"Tough times don't last but tough people do."
~ Robert H. Schuller

When we hit the tough times it can be hard to push through, but here's the thing: if we put our big boy/girl pants on and fight with everything we have, we can make it.

- We can try setting a goal to read one chapter from a personal development book every day.
- We can make sure we drink plenty of water to keep us hydrated.
- We can make sure we are eating well and getting the right amount of sleep.
- We can have a 1:1 with a positive person to help dilute the negatives.

Ultimately, as the *Kobe Bryant* quote says, we need to adjust and stop whining, stop complaining and get on with it.

For those of you who run your own businesses, I know its tough. I have been through 3 recessions and one thing I can absolutely guarantee is that if it won't kill you, it will make you stronger.

Times are changing - constantly - which means we can't keep running our businesses in the same old way. We need to adapt to change, to look at alternative ways to work so that when the tough times come we will be more resilient and more prepared.

Adapting isn't failing. Adapting allows us to build better businesses that are more able to handle the bad days and be more flexible when flexibility is required. Think about the COVID-19 pandemic for a moment, and how so many companies had to adapt to allow their staff to work from home simply to survive.
It hit so many businesses incredibly hard but those who were able to adapt, were more unscathed than those who could not.

I've said in many of these articles that it's important to ask for help and I cannot stress this enough. Once we stop trying to be all things to all people we instantly make our businesses more flexible and open to change. And if you don't know where to go for help then start networking. You will be surprised at how much help there is out there for business owners.

Consider, for example, collaborative working. Who do you know who runs a similar business to you? Look at ways of working *with* them rather than viewing them as a competitor.

Review your client base - how strong is it? Are there clients who used to spend money with you and are no longer spending?

Look at your suppliers and talk to other suppliers. Can you trim costs anywhere?

Think about the cost of your lifestyle. Are you driving a more expensive car than you need, for example? If so, who are you trying to impress?

We all need to be looking at our business as if it were part of the family and make sure we look after it - *because if we look after our business, it will look after us*

Whereas if we abuse our businesses, the outcome will only ever be negative. Refusing to change and adapt is a risk we take at our own peril.

If you want to get through the tough times then put those big pants on, stop whining and adjust.

Get out there and make things happen.

~ ~ ~ ~

~ 45 ~

DO YOU CREATE SUCCESSFUL HABITS?

"Successful people are simply those with successful habits."
~ Brian Tracy

How good are you at creating successful habits in your business? If this is something you fall short on then, you need to read *The 7 Habits of Highly Effective People* by *Stephen Covey*. In fact, read it anyway, regardless. Every single business owner should read this book. What follows is *my interpretation* of these habits.

Habit 1 ~ BE PROACTIVE - I began to understand that if I simply reacted to every situation, I wouldn't survive in business for long. I realised that I needed to embrace a more proactive stance. I needed to be able to adapt to change, over and above what I was already doing because if I was doing the same thing as the previous year, I was probably going backwards.

Habit 2 ~ BEGIN WITH THE END IN MIND - This I interpreted as having a 'why', a reason for doing what I was doing. I decided to review my goals, short and long-term so that I could plot the journey to my 'why'. I evaluated what I wanted and when I wanted it so that I knew exactly what my end goal was. I set a date for my goals as well, so that I could maintain my vision and direction.

Habit 3 ~ PUT FIRST THINGS FIRST - This habit involved looking at the list of tasks I had and deciding what was *important to do* as opposed to what I *wanted to do*. This was uncomfortable when I was faced with tasks I would rather put off but this habit helped me to realise that it was the urgent, important and often challenging tasks which would move me and my business forward.

Habit 4 ~ THINK WIN WIN - When I was networking, I would look to pass referrals to others as often as I could. What this habit taught me was that in order to create successful partnerships with others, there needs to be a win-win mentality on both sides. I remember years ago passing a successful referral to someone for a large conservatory for tens of thousands of pounds. They gave me a bottle of wine as a thank you. They never got another referral from me because they had won, but I had lost. There was no win-win.

Habit 5 ~ SEEK FIRST TO UNDERSTAND, THEN TO BE UNDERSTOOD - One thing I have always tried to be is a great communicator. I truly believe in the adage of having two ears and one mouth for a reason. It's so easy to fall into the habit of talking - especially during awkward silences - however this habit reminded me that we are always at our most effective when we are actively listening. Most people do not listen with the intent to understand, they listen with the intent to reply. Listening with the intent to reply means you are not really listening; you are only actively listening when your intent is to understand. Someone once gave me a powerful quote by *Stephen R. Covey*: *"To know and not do to, is not to know."*

Habit 6 ~ SYNERGISE - In the early days of my business, I instinctively understood that I needed to be a collaborator and encourage creative cooperation between myself and other business owners. When I dug deeper into the 'synergise' habit, I realised that it resonated with the way I worked. For me it was all about looking for opportunities to work with others to create a mutual benefit - not only to both business parties, but also to the end client. These were lessons I gained from my first network marketing program. I believe it's about doing the right thing rather than looking to line your own pocket first.

Habit 7 ~ SHARPEN THE SAW - I used this habit as a reminder to continue repeating all of the previous habits. Instead of thinking I could 'do something once' and it would be fine, I made myself return to the previous habits over and over again. And repeat. Doing something once in business is never enough, so working on ourselves and our business via this self-renewal process is a no-brainer. For me it has solidified balance in both my work and personal lives.

I cannot recommend *The 7 Habits of Highly-Effective People* by *Stephen Covey* enough. I have barely scratched the surface with my thoughts on each habit. The only way you can really make this work for you is to grab a copy and start applying the principles in the same way that I did.

It might feel like a lot, but I took the process step by step, reviewing my own business with honesty during each habit and didn't put undue pressure on myself.

The best part is that once you've created a habit, it's there to stay.

~ 46 ~

DO YOU FEEL LIKE YOU ARE GOING 'UP' THE 'DOWN' ESCALATOR?

"Worrying gets you nowhere. If you turn up worrying about how you're going to perform, you've already lost. Train hard, turn up, run your best and the rest will take care of itself."
~ Usain Bolt

Do you feel like you are going **up** the **down** escalator in life, working as hard as you can and getting nowhere?

You are not alone. There are so many people in life who feel like this, so the question is: *how long are you going to keep doing things the way you are doing them?* Because if you keep going the way you are, you'll keep getting nowhere. You'll never get off the down escalator.

In life and business there will inevitably be times when you feel like you're busting your gut and going backwards - the key when you experience these times is to just keep going. Think about it, even if you are taking three steps forward and two steps back, you're still moving forward one step, it's just going to take a little longer to reach your destination.

As the quote from Usain Bolt says, don't worry about it - worrying will get you nowhere. You have to stay focused, keep positive, and make the best of every day.

This is where a positive attitude really helps and an easy way to achieve this is by reading personal development books. You can also reach out to a mentor or someone you trust, someone who believes in you and your business to help get back onto a positive trajectory. Even simply picking up the phone to a friend or family member can make a huge difference.

Plan your days and make sure you take at least an hour out for yourself to go for a walk, or have a break from technology. This break is hugely important for your mind plus it allows you time to think and process the day thus far.

Most business owners I know spend far too little time working ON their business because they are too wrapped up on working IN the business. Working ON your business (i.e. doing the things that will move your business forward) should make up at least 10% of your work week.

It is vital to your longevity and its importance is often overlooked.

Businesses that fail often lack planning. Owners and employees will turn up at the office and literally plough through the days work, with no forward planning which means no working ON the business. It's only at this point often, we start to look at what has gone wrong by which time, it's too late.

> *"There are the few who make things happen, the many more who watch things happen, and the overwhelming majority who have no notion of what happens."*
> *~ Nicholas Murray Butler*

We need to be in the 'few who make things happen' but we can only be there if we are spending time working ON our businesses and planning - consistently. One of the biggest frustrations I have with most small business owners is they literally wait for the shit to hit the fan before they do something about it - by which time it is far too late. The demise of so many businesses is because of this. DO NOT let it happen to you.

To me, running a business is simple - well, tough but simple:

1. Stop being all things to all people. Do what you are good at and outsource everything else.
2. Build a strong team of outsourced professionals around you - make sure you check their credentials first though - and meet with those professionals at least once a month to make sure you are on track.
3. Make sure you have a mentor who is there to support you and will do what's right for you rather than simply lining their own pockets.

You've got this!

~ ~ ~ ~

~ 47 ~

DO YOU MAKE EXCUSES?

"Ninety-nine percent of the failures come from people who have the habit of making excuses."
~ George Washington Carver

"I can't do that because I am too busy".

"I wont be able to make that event because I have too much work on".

I've probably heard every possible excuse over the last 40 years of being in business and, whilst there are genuine reasons for us being unable to do certain things, sometimes we are (all) guilty of making an excuse.

Harmless? Well, no, especially not in business. In my experience, making too many excuses can put you on the fast-track line to failure.

A couple of years ago I set myself a goal to walk 10,000 steps every day which, on the face of it, sounded doable but let me tell you, there were many days I could easily have made excuses not to get out and walk. I knew, though, that if I continued to find excuse after excuse, any habit I had built would disappear along with all of the benefits I was reaping.

Someone once told me a long time ago: *"You can make money or you can make excuses - you can't do both."*

Which is so true. I really do not accept excuses from myself or clients I work with because I know how damaging they can be to our attitude and ultimate success.

When faced with difficult times, it's easy to make excuses for poor performance or poor decisions or lack of sales etc. however sadly, it is those businesses who make such excuses that usually end up folding. Business owners who don't accept excuses, though, and continually look for opportunities will, more often than not, thrive.

Having a business mentor on your team - in my opinion - is vital for ultimate success and will help you to avoid those excuses. A mentor will be an investment that will pay dividends with their support. Those who mentored me throughout my career have helped me to stay on track, picked me up when I was down and were there simply to listen. When times are tough, it's so important to have someone to offer encouragement.

I've mentioned it in many of these articles, but I really do recommend reading *"The E Myth Revisited"* by *Michael Gerber*. This book will teach you how to run your business properly.

Please be aware of using external circumstances as an excuse **not** to do something. We cannot control external circumstances, we can only control ourselves and our reaction to these so, however frustrating or upsetting these circumstances might be, we have to look beyond them and focus on what we **can** do rather than what we **can't**. Taking this kind of control makes us stronger, more resilient and able to handle future issues that will arise.

Many business owners will blame a recession for their businesses failure, but even this is mostly an excuse. Recessions are tough, no two ways about it, but usually they aren't the catalyst. Instead they're the final nail in the coffin of a business which has lacked previous positive action.

> *"We are exactly where we have chosen to be."*
> *~ Vernon Howard*

Where we are **today** is a result of the decisions we made in the **past**. Where we are **tomorrow** will be a result of the decisions we make **today**.

Make sure the decisions you make are **wise decisions** and not **excuses**.

~ ~ ~ ~

~ 48 ~

HOW DO NEGATIVE SITUATIONS AFFECT YOUR ATTITUDE?

"Attitude is a little thing that makes a big difference."
~ Winston Churchill

External negative circumstances can really affect our attitudes - right?

We've all been in situations that feel as if the whole world is against us and these will almost certainly affect our attitude. What we need, therefore, are people around us who can pull us through these dark times. Not only that, we need to try to find the opportunities in every situation though often, as business owners, we are too 'close' to the situation to see any and this is where are cheering squad come in.

I was once advised that, at the end of every year, I should split the people I had spent time with that year into three categories:

Category 1 - those we've spent a lot of time with who we consider to be close friends or associates BUT who drain our positivity. The people in this category at the end of each year are those we should limit spending time with or disassociate from ourselves completely.

Category 2 - these are people we do not spend a lot of time with but every time we see them we feel energised. They have a huge positive influence on our lives and so we need to be spending more time in their company.

Category 3 - covers those we consider to be 'good friends', yet we always feel better when we leave their company than we do when we are with them. This is another category of people with whom we should limit our time.

At the end of the recent global pandemic, I made a point of reviewing my contacts in this way and gained a much clearer perspective on who I should be spending time with.

You don't only need to do this once, though. You should do it annually at least, although there's nothing wrong with doing it more often. It really is illuminating and once you've got into the habit of categorising your contacts in this way, I guarantee everyone who comes into your life from that moment forth will subconsciously be categorised. The beauty of this is that you will automatically start spending the right time with the right people and these are the ones who will have a positive influence in your life and business. They will always see the good, recognise the opportunities and uplift you.

Social media has a part to play, too. I see many posts on various platforms which have a negative (business) bias and I often feel that those posting should not be saying what they are given the job/position/business they are in. Remember, we all leave a digital footprint and the last thing we want is for our potential clients and customers to see us spreading negativity.

Winston Churchill summed it up perfectly when he said: *"Attitude is a little thing that makes a big difference"*.

The impact a positive attitude has on ourselves and the people around us is huge. When I was younger I did not have a positive attitude, but when I began networking and associating with successful and success minded people, that began to change. I read business and personal self-development books like they were going out of fashion and my car was turned into a mobile university, littered with positive audio tapes.

The effect it had on me was so profound that I decided to introduce my children to these audio tapes from an early age. My hope was that they would avoid (or at least cope better with) the negative years. Even though they may not have fully understood the intricacies at the time, they were absorbing that same positivity I was and I genuinely believe it helped them to get where they are today.

Our legacy is important and I firmly believe we should leave behind a positive and 'can do' attitude. The way we treat people is way more important than any money we might bequeath.

~ ~ ~ ~

~ 49 ~

HOW DO YOU COPE WITH SETBACKS?

"Success is not final, failure is not fatal; it is the courage to continue that counts."
~ Winston Churchill

For this article I am thrilled to collaborate with my good friend Marlena O'Donnell, who is one of the most resilient people I have ever met. Resilience is one of the most important characteristics we need as small business owners because there is one thing that is almost as certain as death and taxes - and that's that we will encounter setbacks.

Setbacks, though, are actually part of the growth curve. Generally we learn more from failure than we do from success – as long as we don't keep making the same mistake.

The biggest business challenge I faced was the 2008/9 recession. My business partner had left the previous year so I was facing it on my own. I remember my accountant coming in to see me a couple of months before year end in April 2009. If May 2009 was as bad as April 2009, he said, I'd have to shut up shop.

After he'd left I allowed myself a 30-minute mild panic before realising I had to get a grip of myself. I called a meeting with the other three members of my team and between us we put some plans in place to help us get through the crisis. Each of us dug deep and by becoming increasingly resilient, we survived.

For the rest of this article, I will hand over to Marlena O'Donnell for her insightful thoughts on resilience.

Note: Marlena's input was given during the COVID-19 pandemic, so it is to this (pandemic) she refers.

"We all need resilience both in business and personal life. Resilience is not something we develop or strengthen - we are all built for resilience. When we believe that we can achieve something, we will take actions to towards it, but when we become overwhelmed by fear and insecurity, we stop trusting our own resilience and don't take actions to help us handle a particular challenge.

Right now, we are finding ourselves in unfamiliar territory. We do not know what is going to happen and what the new norm will look like. It may feel as if we are not in control. And this is true - we are not in control of the circumstances, but we can control our response and take appropriate actions.

Resilience is about not becoming overwhelmed by self-doubt - you have dealt with challenges in the past and you can handle any challenges that will come your way.

If you are not sure how - reach out for help. Remember - you are not on your own. Seek help if you do not know how to move forward.

You can always take action - baby steps are better than no steps. Be persistent - sometimes, we do not immediately see the results of what we do, but being consistent and persistent will eventually bring you results. Keep going, no matter what. If you freeze, you will be moving back. Take actions based on reality and not emotions or self-judgement. We don't know what the future holds, but this should not stop us from taking care of ourselves and our business to ensure the best possible outcomes.,,

~Marlena O'Donnell

~ 50 ~

HOW GOOD ARE YOU AT ADAPTING?

"It is not the strongest of the species that survive, nor the most intelligent, but the one most responsive to change."
~ Charles Darwin

Adapting and evolving is part of life. Adapting in business is no different. Being responsive to change is vitally important to continued success. If you are standing still and doing the same things this week, this month, this year then you are probably going backwards. If what you have been doing for the last X number of years is not working or giving you what you want, then why are you still doing it?

From my own personal experience, what we were initially doing at the inception of our business in 1987 was vastly different to what we were doing when the business was sold in 2016. During this time we had evolved into an Advertising Agency, even though we never set up to be one. At the time of conception we were only selling advertising space which we continued to do for over 30 years, but the business changed so much.

Our first evolution was additionally moving into the outdoor advertising sector. We began offering five services which grew to over fifty services. We evolved our company structure, too; from a business partnership we became co-directors as our company evolved to become a limited entity. After that, in 2007 when my business partner left, I ran it alone with the support of my amazing team. Throughout the whole of this time we experienced massive changes which we recognised were necessary in order not only to survive, but also to thrive.

The question to ask yourself is this: what are *you* doing to adapt and evolve or are you still doing the same thing you did when you started the business?

If you have never read *"Who Moved my Cheese"* and *"Out of the Maze"* by *Dr Spencer Johnson*, I highly recommend you do. They are the best books I have ever read on change and how to adapt.

Though you might understand the need to evolve and adapt, I'd like to illustrate why it is crucial by using three real-life examples of companies local to me who were unable to adapt. Ultimately, for each of them, it resulted in their businesses failing.

1. <u>Drews the Ironmongers</u> - 87 years in business and 4 generations. Closed January 2019.

   They blamed external circumstances. The press report stated:

   "We have traded in Reading for 87 years but unfortunately the costs of running a bricks and mortar business now dominated by internet merchants mean that it is no longer a viable business."

2. <u>Carters Outdoor Sports Clothing</u> - 200 years in business. Closed December 2019

   They blamed external circumstances, however they did not move into the online space until 2017. This compares to Amazon who began selling products online in 1995. Carters' Operations Manager confirmed:

   "The business has had to close due to changing shopping habits".

3. <u>Newmans Shoe Shop</u> - 126 years in business. Closed in February 2020.

   A company report stated that closure was inevitable because it was *'not possible to compete in a global market.'*

One similarity between theses "excuses" is the growth of internet marketing but, if you look at their timelines you can see that each of these companies came to the online game far too late.

Whilst I cannot speak to exactly what happened, I am almost certain they would have seen the trends and noticed their impact on the marketplace. By not reacting or adapting in time, they found themselves on the back foot and when push came to shove, unable to save their businesses. The lesson to be learned here is that in business *we have to be proactive rather than reactive We have to be masters of our destiny not creators of our downfall*

It is my belief that in order for any business to survive (and thrive), a sensible mix of offline and online marketing activity needs to be in place. We need to make sure we keep the "human" element to our business and remain approachable whilst also offering 'quick fixes' online. All of this should be underpinned by great service and relationships which is key to ongoing business success.

~ ~ ~ ~

~ 51 ~

HOW STRONG ARE YOUR COMMITMENTS?

"When you make a commitment you build hope.
When you keep it, you build trust."
~ Stephen M. R. Covey

Whenever we begin a new year, often we make commitments to ourselves; things that we will ensure we do in the months and year ahead.

At the start of 2020, I made a commitment to write an article every week of the year - and I achieved that.

I also made a commitment to post a positive message each day throughout 2020 and I achieved that, too.

Though these were commitments I made to myself, it went deeper than that. I wanted to commit to other business owners that I would pass on my knowledge and experience in the hope it would help them on their own business journey.

This commitment (to other business owners) led me to make a further pledge in 2021 to continue writing weekly articles and daily positive messages. Because I was able to draw on my own personal experience for these articles and messages, I felt sure I would be able to continue to add value and support to those around me.

This book is the culmination of those commitments. Having delivered over 100 articles through social media, I wanted my support to be available on a wider scale which meant my next commitment was to put all of these articles together in one place along with any appropriate and/or beneficial resources.

At the end of the day, I have been in the business world for over 40 years, so I am certain I will have something to offer every business out there. Getting these articles to a larger audience is now my ultimate goal.

What commitments have you made for your business? Think about the next twelve months and what they might look like. What can you do, or what can you commit to do that will help you build a better and more sustainable platform?

Also ask yourself what commitments you can make to help colleagues or networking buddies. What can you do or offer that will increase their business presence and stability.

The concept of commitments also goes beyond business. What commitments are you going to make to your life partner or your children to make sure this coming year is better than the previous year?

This is the point where you need to remind yourself that *you* are in total control of you. This includes your attitude and *how* you react to particular situations. We know that as hard as we may want to try, it is impossible for any of us to control external circumstances or situations *but* what we *can* control is our *reaction* to these.

When it comes to honouring commitments, you are generally only going to be able to do this if these commitments have come from your *own decisions and thoughts*.

Note: if you need to seek help to achieve these commitments, then do so. Do not ever feel you are alone, because you are not.

There are lots of people out there willing to help because we are all in the journey of life together. Remember:

- We all need each other.
- Life is so much better if we all get along.
- We are entitled to have a difference of opinion from others.
- But don't fall out with someone because you have a different opinion.
- These differences make the human race what it is today.

~ ~ ~ ~

~ 52 ~

OPTIMIST OR PESSIMIST?

"A pessimist sees difficulty in every opportunity; an optimist sees the opportunity in every difficulty."
~ Winston Churchill

"Optimism is the best way to see life."
(LOLzombie.com)

Success in life and business does not go in a straight upward line. There are always ups and downs and bumps along the way. On countless occasions people have said to me, "*It must be great to run your own business*," or "*You are so lucky*". Well, yes, it is great to run your own business, but others only ever see the successes, they don't see the failures. The same is true of luck.

Gary Player (golfer), famously said: "*The more I play golf, the luckier I get*".

Which is a bit like being in business.

- ✓ We have to have a positive attitude.
- ✓ We need to be optimistic.
- ✓ We always have to look for new opportunities.
- × But sometimes it is difficult.

✓ Being around successful or success minded people is a great way to keep your mind right.
✓ So is plugging into a personal development programme.

Being a small business owner or a solopreneur can be a very lonely place. Having networked for over 30 years, I sometimes assume that every small business owner has access to a large number of contacts, yet more often than not, they don't. Only a very small percentage of business owners network yet without networking, we will never build up our contact base. Nor will we discover *what* we don't know and *who* we don't know.

Unfortunately our brains are wired to have a negative bias, so it can be hard to remain optimistic simply by the nature of being human. If we add to that a lack of support network or others to bounce ideas off, then keeping up a level of positivity becomes even more challenging.

The fact is: **we don't see the opportunities that someone who is not directly involved with our business will see.**

Therefore, networking for me, is a complete no-brainer. In addition, I've curated a few tips here that can help us to remain optimistic:

1. 'Try On' a Positive Lens - Do this by feeding your brain only positive material.
2. Take Note of the Company You Keep - Hang around only positive and upbeat people.
3. Turn Off the News - If you want to go to bed and wake up negative, watching the news before bed will achieve this goal.
4. Write in a Journal for a Few Minutes Each Day - Note down Positive Thoughts and Action Plans, along with Goals and Dreams.
5. Acknowledge what you Can and Cannot Control - We cannot control external circumstances.
6. Acknowledge the Negative - Recognise it because it is out there, and then dilute it with Positivity.
7. **Above All: Don't Try To Do This On Your Own** - Seek help and support from others, especially when you are not feeling particularly optimistic.

The issues and problems/challenges we have in our business will not be solved with the same mindset that created them, so we need to look to others. Those outside of your business will offer a fresh-perspective and may even uncover a solution you have not considered. Don't be afraid to ask other business owners or business connections for help.

Note: If you have to pay for this help, check the credentials of those you are asking, and remember to look at it as in investment in you and your business as opposed to an unwelcome cost.

~ ~ ~ ~

~ 53 ~

TRUST

"TRUST - takes years to build, seconds to break and forever to repair."
~ Dhar Mann

Many of my articles are based on personal experiences and how those experiences made me feel. Underpinning everything, for me, is TRUST.

We all need to be trusted and we need to trust others in pretty much every aspect of our lives:

- IN BUSINESS - as a leader, employee or business owner

   Whether you work for someone else or you work for yourself it's pretty much the same.

   » You need to **trust** your work colleagues to do what they say they will do.
   » If you are the **leader** of a team or a **business owner**, you need to **lead by example**.
   » Someone once said to me, "*It's what you do when no one is watching that is your true character*". So true!
   » You need to be able to **trust** your **suppliers** to deliver the product or service when they say they are going to.
   » Your **suppliers** need to **trust** you; that your request is detailed correctly and that you will pay on time for example.
   » Your **customers** need to **trust** you will deliver the product or service they have paid for and on the due date.
   » You need to **trust** your **customers** to be honest and to pay you on time.

   Too many people in business abuse the trust laid upon them by lying or passing the buck on to someone else.

- IN LIFE - as a parent, family member or friend

   » We all think we can trust our families - and we should be able to - but far too often I hear stories of people who can't.
   » We need our family members to trust us.
   » We need friends we can trust and who can trust us.
   » Without trust it is very difficult to live a healthy life - mentally and physically.

» We need to have the mentality that we are the most trustworthy people we know.

» If we have a partner, they need to be able to trust us. Without that trust it will be difficult to have a wholesome relationship because there may always be a hint of doubt.

» Our kids need to trust us and if we act in the right way around them, the hope is that they will be the same to others. My close friends are like family to me.

» We trust each other by our actions and the way we conduct ourselves.

- AS A COUNTRY

Lets look at the wider picture.

As a country or a nation, we have to be able to trust the leaders of those countries. What happens if we don't trust them any more?

This is when we begin to see real problems in society.

Personally I think trust in politicians is at the lowest it has ever been, yet our countries are run by these representatives. If we are losing trust in our politicians, then surely we are walking a dangerous tightrope when it comes to the evolution and success of our countries'?

~ ~ ~ ~

WHAT DO WE SAY WHEN WE TALK TO OURSELVES?

"We all talk to ourselves. A major key to success exists in what we say
to ourselves which helps to shape our attitude and mindset."
~ Darren Johnson

How powerful is self talk? What is meant by self talk?

I remember reading a book many years ago called, *"What To Say When You Talk To Yourself,"* by *Shad Helmstetter*. This book was written in 1982 - over 40 years ago - and the content is still valid today.

Fact: We all talk to ourselves - all of the time.

But what are we saying? Are we portraying negative thoughts and self talk?

With our brains genetically wired to have a negative bias, the chances are that we are. However, remember here that much of the self-talk 'input' comes from social media, news channels and the press, so firstly, it's not a case of (only) blaming ourselves and secondly, this is a great argument for reducing our exposure to these external sources.

Regardless of where our negative input originates, it's important that we dilute this negative by taking control of our lives and what goes into our brains and thoughts.

"Garbage in, garbage out."

Popularised in the early days of computing, this phrase was shortened to GIGO and was used to describe the input of flawed or poor quality data to any given computer system leading to a subsequent resultant poor quality or flawed output. If you put garbage in, you get garbage out.

Considering that our brains are the most complex and advanced computers on the planet, it therefore follows that putting negative data into our brains will be damaging and counter-productive to everything else that we do.

What we say when we talk to ourselves affects us in many ways:

- It affects how we perform on a day to day basis in our businesses.
- It affects what we eat and how good our mental and physical health is.
- It affects how we respond to every situation and conversation we have.

So, how do we change our thinking and our self talk?

Speaking from a personal perspective (and having been involved in a personal development programme since 1982), I know how much difference having a positive mindset made to my business and life success. Though a note of caution here: *It is not something we can expect instant changes from, but we have to start somewhere.*

How do we start?

1. Start NOW!
2. Read personal development books.
3. Listen to motivational audio books.
4. Hang around with people who have a positive mindset.
5. Exercise care in what you are watching on television/social media etc.
6. Try programmes that will educate, such as documentaries.
7. Search for podcasts which can improve health and mental well being.

There are countless ways - these are just a few to get you going.

Through necessity we have all spent a lot more time indoors over recent years, meaning that it has been hard for some of us to get back into the habit of socialising, yet, however much we love our home environment and however happy it makes us, we also need external input.

Being around others with similar interests/businesses (via networking for example) can be a great way to beat negative self-talk, and what's more, if you're having a laugh at the same time, you cannot be entertaining negative thoughts. As with our bodies', we must feed our brains with "food" that improve us.

I recommend reading *Shad Helmsetter's* book because it provides simple but profound techniques that will help you to regain control of your brain's input. By learning how to talk to yourself in new ways, you will notice a dramatic improvement in every area of your life.

~ ~ ~ ~

~ 55 ~

YOU ARE NOT GOING TO GET OUT OF LIFE ALIVE

"All of life is a risk; in fact, we're not going to get out alive. Casualness leads to casualties. Communication is the ability to affect other people with words."
~ Jim Rohn

We all know we are not going to get out of life alive, so maybe it's worth thinking about what we (will) have done to leave this world in a better place than when we arrived.

Each of us has our own belief system; I believe that we need to live our lives with strong morals and ethics and that we should always put people ahead of personal wealth or material possessions.

Think of it this way: *We all have the ability to touch other people's lives.*

It doesn't have to cost money to touch someone's life. There is a principle I love to promote known as 'paying it forward', where we can offer to help (in whatever small way) improve the quality of life for another person. This could be personal or business. The end goal is to put a smile on their face.

I wanted to build my business and brand around doing the right thing - looking after my clients and suppliers and ensuring a long and harmonious business relationship - which is something I believe every one of us should aspire to.

One of the benefits of working for ourselves is that we have the ability to pick and choose who we do business with. Life is too short to be working with clients or suppliers who are a constant drain on us. To thrive we need to be with those who have the same values as us, people we know we can trust. People who could do business with us (and vice versa) on a handshake with no repercussions if it doesn't work out.

It's about making life and business as pleasurable as we can and much of that circles back to *trust* which is something I have covered in other articles.

I have always said that anyone who doesn't conduct their life with the right values will find those values coming back to bite them at some point in their life.

What you give, you get back in my opinion, so make sure you do good.

Being in business for ourselves is an exciting adventure, and will be a much more pleasurable experience if we build a good team around us. This not only includes any staff we employ, but also relates to those we outsource to. By focusing on what we know we are good at and getting help for all the other stuff, we will enjoy the day to day operation of our business so much more.

DON'T:

- **Overwork** - don't think that working 70 or 80 hours a week means you are running a good business - its quite the opposite and it will affect other areas in your life.

DO:

- Make sure you have a **mentor** - someone who has been where you are and where you strive to be. A good mentor will ask you questions, test you and help you move forward.
- **Build a better** business **before** you build a **bigger** business.
- Treat your **business as one area of your life**. Care for it the same as you care for your family, partner, children and friends.
- **Don't abuse** your business.
- Make sure **you own** the business and that the business **does not own you**.
- Build your business on **solid foundations** by getting **help and support**. Look at this as an investment in your business.
- Make sure you work with **people you can trust** and **people who trust you**.
- Do what you **say** you are going to do.
- **Always keep** those **communication** channels open.

Leave this life all the better for you having been here.

~ ~ ~ ~

56

ARE YOU BORN TO STAND OUT OR JUST FIT IN?

"The world says fit in; the universe says stand out."
~ Matshona Dhliwayo

- »   Be a Lion, not a Sheep.

- »   Be a critical thinker, not a conformist.

- »   Be a maverick.

- »   Be a disruptor - continually ask questions.

- »   Be courageous, not a coward.

We were born to stand out, we were not born to fit in. We are all individuals. We all have our own minds - if only we use them. **We** control us. No one else has that right or authority unless you allow them, and you should never go down that road.

As business owners we should all be Lions, critical thinkers, mavericks, disruptors and courageous. If we wanted to follow the crowd, we would never have stepped outside that bubble of mediocrity. We would have forever remained a Sheep.

It's funny how many business owners fit the description of being a Lion, but when it comes to personal decisions, they very much follow the sheep.

Why would you do that?

Is it because someone in authority tells you to do it, or the media tells you to do it, or because you get criticised if you don't follow the crowd?

> *Don't forget, you are in charge of your own mind - and only you*
> *Why would you let someone else take control?*

I have been on this planet for 68 years and have spent 43 of those in complete control of my life, my finances and the decisions I make. Having that control has taught me so much.

Trust is one of the biggest human traits, yet often, depending on where we put that trust, it can leave us disappointed. Perhaps we don't receive something promised by a colleague or supplier, perhaps payments are not made in good faith and on time, or perhaps decisions are taken by those we trust that don't work for us as an individual, a business owner or as a wider society.

The only way we can overcome this and retain control is to continually ask questions. It won't, in my experience, benefit any business owner to simply accept what they are being told. We have to keep asking questions of those we trust and those around us, otherwise we can never know exactly what is right for us. Trust your instincts and don't follow the crowd.

Remember: **WE WERE ALL BORN TO STAND OUT.**

NOW IS THE TIME TO DO IT.

~ ~ ~ ~

4 Section Four

Running A Successful Business

57.	BEGIN WITH THE END IN MIND
58.	ARE YOU AWARE OF BUSINESS TRENDS?
59.	CHOICES - HOW IMPORTANT ARE THEY?
60.	BUSINESS IS NOT A TEMPLATE
61.	BUSINESS IS NOT THE SAME - WE NEED TO LEARN
62.	DO YOU LET YOUR CIRCUMSTANCES DEFINE YOU?
63.	HINTS AND TIPS FOR SMALL BUSINESSES
64.	HOW LUCKY DO YOU FEEL?
65.	LOOK AT YOUR SUPPLIERS AS PART OF YOUR TEAM
66.	PEOPLE BUY FROM PEOPLE
67.	RELIABILITY
68.	REST IF YOU MUST, BUT DON'T QUIT
69.	HOW DO YOU RUN A SUCCESSFUL BUSINESS?
70.	TECHNOLOGY IS AN ADDITION TO THE HUMAN RACE, NOT A REPLACEMENT
71.	UNDER PROMISE, OVER DELIVER
72.	WHAT HAVE WE LEARNED FROM SITUATIONS OUTSIDE OF OUR CONTROL?
73.	ARE YOU TOP OF MIND?

57

BEGIN WITH THE END IN MIND

"To begin with the end in mind means to start with a clear understanding
of your destination. It means to know where you're going so that you
better understand where you are now and so that the steps you take are
always in the right direction."
~ Stephen Covey

The *Stephen Covey* quote above is from his book *"The Seven Habits of Highly Effective People"* which is a book I highly recommend to anyone in business.

Understanding how to goal-set properly and make sure you stay on track is vitally important for success in anything you do:

- You have to look at where you currently are, decide where you want to be and by when.
- Work backwards from the end goal. This will give you the steps you need to take to ensure you stay on track.
- You must have an end goal with a date or you will aimlessly drift from one day and one week to another.

The easiest way for me to explain this is to use a real life example:

In April 2003, after watching the London Marathon, I decided I wanted to run the 2004 event with a couple of friends.

> The event was taking place on the 18 April 2004, which was set in stone. Any training I did had to be done with this date in mind. If I did not train sufficiently within that timescale, I would not be able to complete the race or I would end up quitting and not running it at all. Quitting is not a part of my mindset, though. I have learned over the years that having belief in ourselves is a huge part of achieving our goals.

> At the time of making this decision, I was running 3 miles once a week which I knew was not going to be enough to get me around a marathon course. The problem was, I had never run a marathon before, so the first thing I needed to do was get some advice. I knew

someone who had completed a marathon so I asked him what training I should do and if he had any other useful advice. The first thing he told me to do was buy a decent pair of running shoes and the second thing he advised was to subscribe to the Runners World magazine. This, he assured me, would provide a running plan as well as a diet plan.

I took his advice. The plan went something like this:

About 4 weeks before the Marathon (mid March) I needed to be running a long run of 18 or 20 miles.

About 12 to 24 weeks before the Marathon, I needed to be running a number of half marathons - this meant I had to achieve my first half marathon around September time. The magazine suggested several races I could enter that would work with my training plan.

About 8 weeks before the half marathon in September I needed to be running 10 miles, making the first one of these due around July.

Prior to the 10 mile runs I was to complete several 10k runs (6 miles) which, according to the training plan, I needed to be able to complete about 8 weeks from where I was.

This structure gave me the baby steps to my goal and the first thing I had to do was build up from 3 miles to 6 miles, over the next 8 weeks. I worked out that I would need to have the discipline to run 3 times per week to achieve this, so that's what I did. After that I moved onto the next stage and so on.

I found having an event to enter gave me focus. These were effectively goals within goals which, if I stuck to these and to the plan, I was pretty much guaranteed to be ready for the London Marathon in April 2004.

And I was! I also ran it again in 2005.

I'd found the plan, all I had to do was put it into action and success would be assured.

Setting business goals is exactly the same. *Set them, put them into action, stick to a plan and you will get to where you want to be.*

~ 58 ~

CHOICES ~ HOW IMPORTANT ARE THEY?

"You are free to choose but the choices you make today will determine
what you have, be, and do, in the tomorrow of your life."
~ Zig Ziglar

The choices we make through our lives mould us into who we become, what we do, and the successes we have. In this article, I want to focus on the business choices that we make.

In the 40 + years I was in business, there were 4 recessions - some hitting harder than others. On average, every 10 - 12 years, there will be something (like a recession or a pandemic) that comes along and rocks our boat and our lives.

Anyone who has been in business for a number of years should already have prepared for these eventualities, however it is human nature that some will not have done. Equally new businesses will find it incredibly tough to survive through a recession or similar, so what is the answer?

Planning. Planning is vital.

As the quote from Zig Ziglar says, *"The choices we make today will determine what we have, be and do tomorrow,"* which is applicable to both our personal and business lives. Not only that, we need to be aware that the choices we have made in the past, will have led us to where we are today.

To stay ahead of the game, business owners need to constantly be reinventing themselves and changing the way they do things, or they will be left behind. We live and work in an era of constant change which is exacerbated by the increased use and capability of technology.

If we continue to do the same thing, it is highly likely we will go backwards rather than forwards so it is imperative that we look for new opportunities - always.

I've said it in previous articles, we need to spend time working **ON** our business not just **IN** our business. If you're not sure what the difference is, then here's a quick guide:

Working IN your business, focuses on the day-to-day tasks, e.g.:

- Client projects
- Sales calls
- Accounting and payroll processing
- Maintaining output of services
- Attending meetings or training events

Working ON your business, focuses on strategic and long-term planning and goals, e.g.:

- Ongoing and long-term marketing strategy
- Future product development and advertising
- Business expansion opportunities
- Updating of websites and customer facing information
- Reviewing practices - can these be streamlined?

The other problem with working ON our business, (apart from finding the time to dedicate to it when we are rushed off our feet meeting the day to day needs of being IN our business), is that we are too close to our business to see areas that can be changed, planned or improved upon. That doesn't mean we have created the perfect business model, what it means is that we need to enlist help and advice from outside sources.

There are many excellent resources out there from books to articles which can help you to decide what areas to work ON in your business. A quick internet search will bring up several, so I recommend you do this regularly. Find hints and tips that are achievable and relevant to your business and set aside some time each week (that is non-negotiable) to attend to tasks that will help build your business.

Be IN your business and work ON your business.

This is all part of the planning that I mentioned right at the beginning of this article and it is this planning that will help you and your business to survive the inevitable challenges.

Remember: the choices we make today will shape our tomorrow.

~ 59 ~

BUSINESS IS NOT A TEMPLATE

"Experience is one thing you can't get for nothing."
~ Oscar Wilde

If you know me, you may have heard me make this statement: *"Business is not a template."*

What I mean by this, is that whilst all businesses will encounter some similar issues, there are other challenges which will be unique to our business. We cannot, therefore, use a template to help us run, improve and grow our businesses. We need to find the right solutions and this often means looking outside of our immediate business world.

Bear in mind, often we are the creators of these challenges and problems, so we will not be able to solve them - which is why we call in expert help.

The thing about calling in experts is that they have the experience to identify our weaknesses and support us in finding ways to strengthen these. This may mean we have to pay for an expert trouble-shooter, for example, however I always encourage business owners to look at any monetary payments in this regard as an investment in the future of their business. It is not a cost.

It's perfectly okay to acknowledge that we might need:

• Someone to hold our hand through these challenges.

• Someone to hold us accountable and help us stay on track.

• Someone to help us build a BETTER business - because they have experience along with many dents in their armour which can prevent us from making similar (costly) errors.

• We *can* build a bigger business without support, but remember, if we created the problems, challenges and issues, simply growing our business will not help. All that will do is exacerbate those problems, challenges and issues which may lead to a catastrophic downfall.

• Help to make your business better first - then worry about the next steps.

This is what I have done in the past. I have helped other business owners to work through and overcome any issues/challenges so that they can continue to move forward in their business and achieve their goals.

I remember a conversation I had with someone at a networking event many years ago. After we had introduced ourselves to each other, I asked him what he did, and he told me he was a business coach. I asked him how long he had been doing it and he told me it was his first week, so I asked him what he did last week. He said he was in IT.

What, then, in that scenario, qualified him to be a business coach?

I have met many like this, business owners who lack the experience in their industry to run their own company yet are happy to give advice to others. It's a bit like reading a book. You can't simply read a book and believe that you know everything there is to know about a particular subject/business matter.

Going back to templates for a moment, franchises are a great example of a templated business. In order for a business to be able to become a franchise, there needs to be a repeatable format so that the business can be replicated. Hence, franchises are built on templates. On the basis that there are some excellent franchise opportunities, then it is clear templated business models CAN work. However, if we are a unique business, it is unlikely that following a template exactly, will work for us - BUT, we should build our business as if we were going to franchise it. Why?

Because good franchises have the best systems, and good systems are the strength behind any business.

For more on everything I've mentioned here, I highly recommend reading *"The E Myth Revisited"* by *Michael Gerber*.

~ ~ ~ ~

60

BUSINESS TODAY IS DIFFERENT ~ WE MUST LEARN FROM THE PAST

"Dear Past, thank you for your lessons. Dear Future, I am ready."
~ Snapchamp

Have we *really* learnt from the past?

Are we *really* ready for what is to come?

I suspect there are many business owners who have not learned from their previous mistakes which will only lead to trouble.

Take the COVID-19 Pandemic. The hospitality industry was one of the worst hit and I remember reading an article about a pub who had re-opened for business and experienced over 250 no-shows! People were still getting used to going out again, and understandably, were concerned about being in places such as pubs and restaurants. Now, I'm not suggesting that the pub did anything wrong, but in circumstances were you are relying on good faith, particularly after something as significant as the pandemic, it makes good business sense to consider taking a deposit. At least then they wouldn't have lost out on quite so much business at a time when every penny was crucial.

I firmly believe in taking a deposit, regardless of industry. In my experience, most people don't have a problem with this. If they are genuine, then they want to work with you so paying a deposit does not cause an issue. This simple practice is a great way to secure your business, your income and your sanity.

For over 30 years whilst running my Advertising Agency, I never did business with anyone without a purchase order or some form of payment in advance. To me it didn't make sense not to.

There are business owners who would proudly tell me their figures, their monthly and weekly statistics of how much business they had done. Though I always congratulated them, I also asked if they had been paid.

If their answer was no - which was more often than I would have liked - then I would remind them that unless you have been paid, you can't say that you have done business.

If you have not been paid then you have nothing to show for it other than someone's word which may or may not be reliable. In my view we should all change the way we do business, otherwise we seriously risk our longevity.

Many business owners fall into the trap of thinking that they know it all, yet they are doing the same thing they have always done:

Doing everything themselves and never asking for help.

If we continue to do the same thing day in, day out, yet expect a different result, we are not only fooling ourselves, we will never move forward.

If what you are doing is not working or not working the way you want it to work, DO NOT keep doing it.

Learning from our mistakes is hugely powerful. Often, it is the best way to learn. What is also important, though, is seeking the support of others who can help us to navigate new and difficult times. We are not alone, even though we may feel that we are. I cannot stress enough how important it is to ask for help. Asking for help is a strength, not a weakness.

Being in business for ourselves allows a lifestyle over which we have control. It should also add value to our lives and be a positive influence on who we are as business owners and people.

But, just because we are in business for ourselves, that doesn't mean we have to do everything ourselves. If you need help, find someone who can offer that. It is an investment in your business, you and ultimately, your life.

So learn from the past, be ready for the future. Take control of your life and make sure the lessons learned put you and your business in a far better place than before.

~ ~ ~ ~

61

DO YOU LET YOUR CIRCUMSTANCES DEFINE YOU?

"Don't ever let your circumstances determine your outcome. You are bigger and better than that. You can always control your own destiny. Use what you've got, find what you don't, and make your dreams come true."
~ Gary Vaynerchuk

Do you let your circumstances or what happened in your past define who you are?

Do you let them affect who you are striving to be?

Or, do you raise your head above the parapet and move forward no matter what?

Many people I speak to tell me they do the latter and yet whenever something negative happens, they are down in the dump, seemingly letting the circumstances control them. Often, this leads them straight back to square one and whatever progress they have made will be negated. It is incredibly difficult at this point, to pick up where we left off.

The truth is, there will always been external challenges which threaten to derail us but, no matter how hard it is, we have to keep moving forward otherwise we will spiral ever deeper into a negative mindset.

One of the best ways to stay on track is to surround ourselves with people who can motivate us, who understand our business and goals, who want to see us succeed ... someone like a business coach, for example. A quick phone call or meet up with the right person can almost instantly get us back on track.

During the COVID-19 pandemic, keeping in touch with people outside of our homes occurred via Zoom and similar portals. Whilst this was invaluable in keeping us connected, humans thrive on face to face contact meaning it was important for us to return to meetings and the like as soon as we could.

Since then, Zoom and other online platforms have continued to be used extensively and it is my belief that this has now become too comfortable. Yes, it is time and cost effective, but it keeps us within our comfort zones and, if you've ever read any management or business books, you will know that true growth only happens when we are outside of our comfort zones. If we continue to hide behind screens, even when we don't have to, there is every chance we, and our businesses will get left behind.

When we face circumstances and situations that are outside of our control, we have to accept that these are unavoidable. They will always be there, however, if we look at these as something or someone 'testing' us, then we are far more able to rise to the challenges they present. Look at them this way and you will undoubtedly discover a way to overcome them - even if that means doing nothing. Don't forget that you are not alone either. There are people in your network who will support you and, once you are through the other side you can feel proud of yourself and perhaps even give yourself a reward for surviving (and maybe even thriving!).

It can be hard to believe at times, but we are in control of our own destiny. We have to remember this and surround ourselves with positive influences, which includes making time for our own personal development. We need to have the capability to fulfil the destiny we desire.

If you're not sure where your destiny lies, think about your dreams and where you would like to be. Keep these dreams at the forefront of your mind at all times and maintain the unwavering belief that you will achieve it, not matter what. It's amazing how powerful this simple process can be.

So remember, don't let your circumstances dictate your ultimate outcome. As the quote says, 'use what you've got and find what you don't' - and what you don't have could be hiding in the pages of a business development book or the mind of a friend or mentor. Reach out. Look it up. And reward your success.

~ ~ ~ ~

~ 62 ~

DO YOU THINK YOU ARE LUCKY?

"Luck is what happens when preparation meets opportunity."
~ Seneca

How many times has someone remarked that you were 'lucky'?

It could be for any number of reasons but when it comes to business, do you believe in luck? Or do you think it is down to your attitude, the fact that you seek out opportunities and take them when they come along?

For me it is the latter, although it's important to note here that *we can only take advantage of opportunities if we are prepared for them.*

Lack of preparation is one of the biggest mistakes I see. Business owners will go from job to job, week to week or month to month without any goals or plans. They really don't know where they are going so, if something good happens, you could argue the presence of *luck* in that instance.

Yet I don't believe that any business owner is lucky, it's more about guts. Guts to go out on their own and guts to control their own destiny. Any success a business owner achieves is testament to them having the drive and determination to take control of their destiny, so imagine how much more successful we could be if we took that one step further and introduced *goals* to our businesses. Setting goals and working towards them has multiple benefits but for the purpose of this article, I want to mention two:

1. Goals lead us to being focused on what we want. If we put the appropriate plans in place to achieve these goals, we will always arrive at our end destination - at which time you should be moving the goal posts!

2. Goals lead to positivity which leads to opportunities. If we are on target with our goals, not only will we attract opportunities, we will also have the capacity and planning in place to be able to action these opportunities rather than watch them pass us by.

Hopefully you can see that being in the 'zone' (i.e. working to our goals) enables us to create our own luck. The key to overall success then rests in us remaining in that zone.

Take a moment to consider how prepared you are. Be honest here. If you can't be honest with yourself at this stage you are almost certainly going to struggle further down the line.

Go back to that dream you had - the one that gave you the guts to set up your own business - and revisit the goals you would need to implement to reach that dream.

The dream is your focus, the goals are your mode of transport. Setting goals and working towards them - even if you're only taking baby steps - will always put you way ahead of where you would have been without them.

If you have that dream but have lost sight of how to achieve it, or are just beginning your business journey, here are a few suggestions to get you back on track:

- Build a network of acquaintances and friends who will help and support you.
- Find a mentor.
- Write a business plan and review it regularly.
- Get your finances in order - you cannot build a business for free.
- Set realistic financial goals and review them regularly.
- Know your numbers in all aspects of your business from sales to payroll.
- Expand your knowledge - read personal development books or watch educational videos such as TED talks.

Building a business is like making a cake. These suggestions are your ingredients and, if you forget to add one, your cake won't turn out how you hoped.

Try thinking of your business in this way: *prepare your ingredients* and *plan when to add each one.*

You'll be amazed at how much closer you will be to that ultimate dream goal.

~ ~ ~ ~

~ 63 ~

DO YOU SEE YOUR SUPPLIERS AS PART OF YOUR TEAM?

"Coming together is a beginning; Keeping together is progress;
Working together is success."
~ Henry Ford

Early on in my business life I had a business partner who, when we were meeting with suppliers for lunch, would say that as we were the customer, the suppliers should buy us lunch.

Do you agree with this? Or do you see suppliers as part of your team?

In my experience, most businesses look at their supplier relationships as both different and separate to the relationships with their own team. Yet, if you can imagine what kind of team you would have by including everyone - even suppliers - into that *'team'* mentality, you will see how much stronger all of your relationships will become meaning that, by extension, you will be ahead of your competition.

In business we **need quality suppliers** who look after us **as much** as **we need clients who spend money** with us. We want to ensure longevity with our client base and we should look at those who supply our business in the same way. That's not to say that all suppliers are the same, though.

In my Advertising Agency, for example, we had suppliers that we had to book space with - like when it came to placing an ad on London Underground, there was only one supplier we could approach to achieve this. This meant that *we needed that supplier* more than *they needed us*, so we built our relationship on equal and mutual respect. It didn't matter who bought lunch as long as we maintained a good working relationship.

Suppliers are there to help us, as small businesses, succeed. I have talked at length about the need to outsource in other articles and this is where your relationship with your suppliers, really comes into its own.

If you go to networking events, you will find countless suppliers who can add value to your business.

Remember: *We cannot be all things to all people and we shouldn't even try. Understand what you are good at and outsource everything else.*

At a networking event recently, I was fortunate to listen to a talk by a professional athlete who has eleven European and World titles to her name. During this talk she mentioned how she would regularly get her "TEAM" together – nutritionist, doctor, coach, sports scientist to name a few – to make sure they were all pulling in the same direction. Overall it was *imperative* that they focused on the *same goal* which was to *enable the athlete to achieve success.*

Sometimes the difference between silver and gold can literally be a second or less which is why it is vital for the success of the athlete that her team are all pulling together.

Why, then, should a business be any different?

Here's a suggestion:

If you use (outsource) suppliers like IT, HR, Bookkeeping, Accounting, Business Coach or Mentor, Social Media Marketing etc, why not get them all together once a quarter to make sure you are all pulling in the same direction?

There is an analogy which states that if one horse can pull a ton, two horses together can pull more than twice this amount. This is because the combined force of them pulling together is greater than their individual ability.

Success in business is no different.

~ ~ ~ ~

~ 64 ~

PEOPLE BUY FROM PEOPLE

"People buy from people they know, like or trust."
~ Joel Comm

How good are we (as small businesses) at building relationships?

To me, strong relationships in business are everything. Strong relationships are vital to the success and longevity of business. People buy from people, they do not buy from companies. Building strong relationships and doing what you say you are going to do will build trust and respect and will help you to generate and retain clients.

When I first started in business, someone very successful told me 'not to worry about making money' and 'not to have this as my driving force'. Instead I was told to 'focus on building relationships' and so long as I had a 'product or service in demand', money 'would flow'. I took this advice on board when I started my company in 1987 and it served me well throughout.

Becoming a father further embedded this belief in the value of relationships. The most valuable thing I want to leave behind for my two daughters is a strong sense of values, ethics and morals and the understanding of how beautiful and beneficial the building of long-lasting relationships can be.

My daughters are now both in their thirties and I could not have been more proud when our youngest, Gemma, shared a testimonial she had recently received from one of her customers. As an illustration, I would like to share the email that was sent to Gemma from her manager at John Lewis (department store).

> *"Hi Gemma,*
>
> *I just had to share the experience I have just had on your counter. As I was walking past today I acknowledged a mother and daughter having a look at the VM. I began to help them as much as I could; and the daughter told me about her amazing experience with you last week and how helpful you were, so much so that she had brought her mother in to have a look. Unfortunately you weren't there, but I still managed to*

sell a Zero Foundation and a new launch lip balm. The daughter also purchased a highlighter based on the samples you gave her last week. Immediately afterwards, another lady started speaking to me about wanting a new lipstick and about the fun experience she had with you the other week when trying some new bits and how much of a laugh you'd had together. This also resulted in another sale today.

Gemma, it is clear to see that you are building a very loyal and strong customer base who are experiencing the most outstanding customer service - so much so that they are desperate to return.

Thank you Gemma, I'm so thankful that I got to witness that today, it has made my day.

Keep it up, you are doing an amazing job!"

I am obviously a proud father (!) but I really wanted to share this email to illustrate the appreciation you can receive if you work hard at building relationships with everyone you encounter. Gemma will always have this endorsement in her work and capability which will only help her to flourish as she continues her career.

People buy from people.

So, be that person they want to buy from.

~ ~ ~ ~

RELIABILITY ~ CAN EVERYONE RELY ON YOU TO DELIVER?

"Do what you say you are going to do. People can do nothing but respect that."
~ Steve Harvey

Back when I was in the full flow of running my business, I would refrain from working more than once with anyone who proved themselves to be unreliable.

If we are the buyer, for example, we expect our suppliers to be reliable and to provide the products and services we require - so why should we be any different?

I used to have a great poster in my office which stated:

"It can take months or years to gain a client and seconds to lose one."

How true is that?

Throughout my working life I always strove to provide great service and in return, I expected the same. **If we want to be successful then we must do what we say we are going to do** and, if we cannot deliver, then we need to keep our clients in the loop. Don't leave them in limbo.

If you are a tradesperson and you tell your customer you are going to be round their house at 10am, then to turn up at 3pm is really not acceptable. Firstly that customer may never use your services again and secondly they will tell everybody else. As we all know it is very easy for us to spread good or bad news and it does literally spread like wildfire. So for your own sake and the future of your business make sure the only news being spread about you is good.

If you owe someone money and you cannot afford to pay them, tell them why. They will appreciate you for being honest and be more likely to give you some leeway. During the recession in 2008/9 my business was unable to pay suppliers on their due dates but we always kept in touch and paid part of the invoice, arranging to pay the remainder as soon as we could. This did not deter our suppliers from working with us in the future. They appreciated our honesty and openness which led to a depth of trust which lasted throughout the life of my time in the business and beyond.

Whilst being unable to pay is a tough conversation, if you continue to avoid talking to those to whom you owe money and simply keep promising that you'll pay, then your credibility will go straight down the drain.

I remember a recent conversation with someone who told me that she had a situation with a client who owed her money. That client continually avoided speaking to her and she had (at that time) still not received any payment. Sadly, this is all too common and leads to a very painful lesson which is one we will all, as business owners, inevitably encounter. The point is though, to learn from this by making sure we have processes in place which minimise the chances of people owning us money.

During my time running my business, I was not immune to this, however with each 'bad debt' I took the lessons from it and learned, putting measures in place to protect myself and my business for the next time. In over 33 years, I therefore accrued only five bad debts which totalled less than £10,000.

We can't avoid every pitfall and we can't avoid every bad debt, but what we can do so is make sure that we are reliable, and that we deliver what we say, when we say we will.

Being reliable in EVERYTHING we do is paramount.

~ ~ ~ ~

~ 66 ~

REST IF YOU MUST, BUT DON'T QUIT

"Winners never quit and quitters never win."
~ Vince Lombardi

My apologies, but there is a bit of a rugby theme to this article - hopefully you will indulge me.

I have been a Harlequins season ticket holder for many years and, during the pandemic, access to the games was either not permitted or seriously restricted. I was grateful, therefore, to be able to attend one on Saturday the 26th June 2020 because on that famous day, the Harlequins won the Rugby Premiership Title having faced relegation a mere six months before. It was an incredible turnaround leaving many to ask - what happened?

The answer, was actually simple.

The Harlequins, when faced with relegation, changed their mindset and began to believe that anything was possible.

With the support of their management and supporters they began to pull together as a team unit, worked on their own individual strengths and learned how to explore and employ the strengths of their teammates. In one way, it was as if they *'fell in love with the game'* again, becoming fearless and adopting a *'never say die'* attitude. The chains had been released and, with nothing to lose, they began to play more freely and in a way that they knew they could.

This reminded me of an often quoted poem, *Don't Quit*, which I had displayed on my office wall for many years. I would read it every single day and remind myself that, in the words of *Vince Lombardi*, *'Winners never quit and quitters never win'*.

This attitude is needed in order to be successful in business *but, and this is key, we cannot do it alone*. This has been a theme of many of my articles and it is just as true in this context. The Harlequins had a coach and a manager to support them and keep them on track.

Without someone to keep us accountable and on track in business, it can be so easy to admit defeat and quit.

Every successful sports individual or team has coaches and yet in business, so many business owners try to do everything themselves and think this is the right way to build a business - I can assure you it's not.

We need to do what we are good at doing and focus on our own game, and then build a team of people around us - staff and an outsourced team - who can add quality and experience to make us true "Champions" of the business world. We need to all work together and not be a team of individuals.

Note: You do not need to have the best players in the world to be the best team in the world. You just need have a team of people who are each good at what they do and are able to form a cohesive support network.

Don't Quit

When things go wrong, as they sometimes will,
When the road you're trudging seems all uphill,
When the funds are low and debts are high,
And you want to Smile but have to sigh,
When care is pressing you down a bit,
Rest, if you must, but don't you quit.

Life is queer with its twists and turns,
As every one of us sometimes learns,
And many a failure turns about,
When he might have won if he'd stuck it out,
Don't give up, though the pace seems slow.
You might succeed with another blow.

Often the struggler has given up,
When he might have captured the victor's cup,
And he learned too late, when the night slipped down,
How close he was to the golden crown.

Success is failure turned inside out,
The silver tint of clouds of doubt,
And you never can tell how close you are,
It may be near when it seems afar,
So, stick to the fight when you're hardest hit,
It's when things seem worst that you mustn't quit.

(Attributed to many authors, including Edgar Albert Guest, this poem is available in the public domain. Copyright is not owned or claimed, nor never will it be owned or claimed, by the author of this book)

67

SO, HOW DO YOU RUN A SUCCESSFUL BUSINESS?

"There are no secrets to success. It is the result of preparation, hard work and learning from failure."
~ Colin Powell

Below are a few keys to success based on my 40 + years business ownership experience. Try adopting these - I really want you to succeed!

Key 1:

Associate with successful and success minded people, and always be prepared to learn.

I was fortunate to have been introduced to a personal development programme at the age of 23 which was 7 years before I set up my business. Unbeknown to me, I was getting ready by starting to associate with successful and success-minded people. I began learning what it took to be successful and read personal development books written by those whose achievements I admired. My car became a mobile university as I listened to positive, uplifting and motivational cassettes and CDs. If you haven't started doing this and you are already in business, start NOW!

Key 2:

Look after your staff, clients and suppliers.

If we learnt one thing from the COVID-19 pandemic, it was how important it was to look after our staff. Remember, yes, it is your business, but without your staff you would not be able to function and achieve the success to which you aspire. As a business owner, you need your staff (and suppliers - see previous articles) as much as they need you. A good relationship with your staff is imperative, so look after them well.

Key 3:

Do what you are good at and outsource everything else.

We must understand that, when we set up in business, we do not have all of the skills to succeed. Learn to outsource as early as possible. If you cannot afford to do this from day 1, then start by talking to people and building relationships ready for when you can afford to do so. This also gives you time to check out the credentials of those you would like to outsource to, so that you can make sure they are a good fit for you and your business. They need to be able to deliver the results you require and in my experience, the sooner you find those who are able to do this, the better. It's never great if you are constantly switching from supplier to supplier. And where do you meet these people? Networking. Go networking. Make it part of your marketing activity. This is where you will meet companies that are the right fit for you.

Key 4:

Make sure you always have a handle on the business accounts and finances and know where you stand at any one time.

I read an article once (from the FSB) which stated that 88% of all businesses have no idea where they stand financially at any given moment in time. That's only 12 out of the first 100 people who read this article that knows the financial state of their business. Shocking. I really don't know how the other 88% survive or succeed but I am sure that their businesses will struggle and probably fail. You need to know where you stand financially at all times.

Key 5:

Accept change. It will always be part of our lives. Ignore it at your peril. Refusal to change will kill your business.

We all have to accept that change will be part of everything we do in life and business. We have to plan and prepare for change so that we are in a better position to handle it when it happens. We have to adapt, end of, and refusal to adapt and evolve will kill our business. Visualise 5 years ahead of where you are and put whatever you need in place to reach that vision. Be aware of and open to any opportunities than can positively benefit our business.

Key 6:

Make sure you plan and prepare for every eventuality; there will always be a "What if" that can stop us dead.

Change will always be there, it is a part of our lives, and the best way to cope with change is to learn from our experience. Also, think about people such as suppliers as investments as opposed to a cost. Suppliers are more important to you in the long-term than a short-term revenue deficit. Don't worry about making mistakes - just don't keep making the *same* mistakes. That is insane. Consider your long-term goal and make sure you are preparing for that. Know what you are doing and why. Finally, start with the end in mind. *Why* are you running your business? Without a *why*, the rest is pretty much irrelevant. Discover where you want to be and then work backwards making sure to take baby steps on your return to your goal.

~ ~ ~ ~

68

TECHNOLOGY IS AN ADDITION, NOT A REPLACEMENT

"I fear the day that technology will surpass our human interaction.
The world will have a generation of idiots."
~ Albert Einstein

For this article I am going to use a short-story which, in my opinion, says it better than I ever could. Unfortunately I have been unable to accurately discover the source or author of this story, hence I include it here as an illustrative example only. I do not claim, nor will I ever claim, any copyright or rights to this story. If anyone reading this is aware of its true origins, please let me know so that I can update my reference source accordingly. Thank you.

Technology is an addition to the human race, not a replacement

I spent an hour in the bank with my dad, as he had to transfer some money. I asked him, "Dad, why don't we activate your internet banking?"

"Why would I want to do that?" He asked.

I replied. "You wont have to spend an hour here transferring money. You can even do your shopping online. Everything will be easy!"

I was so excited about initiating him into the online world.

"If I do that," he questioned, "I won't have to step out of the house?"

"No, you won't," I said. "Even groceries can be delivered now and online shops sell everything!"

His answer left me tongue-tied.

"Since I entered this bank today, I have met four of my friends. I have chatted a while with the staff who know me very well. You know I am alone and I need the company. I like to get ready to come to the bank. I make the time because it is the physical contact that I crave."

"Two years back when I got sick, the store owner from whom I buy fruits, came to see me and sat by my bedside and cried. Before your mum died she fell down on her morning walk. Our local grocer saw her, put her in his car and rushed her home because he knew where we lived. Tell me, would I have that 'human' touch if I did everything online? Why would I want everything delivered to me so that the only interaction I had was with my computer?"

I shook my head, momentarily lost for words.

"I like to know the person I'm dealing with," he continued, "not just the 'seller'. This creates bonds and relationships. Can all of that be delivered online as well?"

I chose to say nothing, instead taking on board his final words:

"Spend time with people, son," he said, "not with devices."

Author: Unknown

~ ~ ~ ~

69

UNDER PROMISE, OVER DELIVER

"Quickest way to build trust: Keep promises you make, don't over-promise. Over-deliver, don't under-deliver. If you say you'll do something, make sure you do but if things then run late or go wrong, tell your client at the earliest opportunity."
~ Phil Harding

In my humble opinion and based on my experience, we should **ALWAYS over deliver**. It is one thing I aimed to consistently do in my own business because I recognised that *over-promising* and *under-delivering* was a sure fire way to *destroy client and supplier relationships*.

As a result of adopting this **'under-promise, over-deliver'** approach, I managed to keep my clients and always had a good relationship with them. It was never a big deal to me. It might have meant getting their advertising campaign ready a week early, or securing credit from a supplier due to an issue with a live campaign - this I could then pass onto the client. Whatever it was, I always gave the client more value than they had actually paid for.

If your focus is on **over-delivering**, you will never go far wrong. If your focus is on **over-promising**, though, then you will leave yourself wide open for something going wrong. Your customers (including suppliers) should always be your number one focus - not yourself. Every effort should be put on **delivering a great customer experience** because if you don't do this, you can guarantee that customer will look elsewhere in future.

As the quote says, in order to build trust, keep the promises you make. Don't over-promise. Also, bear in mind what part of that promise you can and cannot control. You should never over-promise on something that is completely outside of your control.

Remember: Trust can take years to build and seconds to lose.

We all need to do the right thing. If we say we are going to do something then we need to do it. It is called responsibility. We have to accept total responsibility for our own actions, and not seek to blame someone else.

If something happens which adversely affects your customer's experience - which it inevitably will at one time or another - never back away from it. Do not ignore it. Deal with it head on, and let the customer know at the earliest opportunity. Your relationship will be stronger if you deal with problems quickly and effectively. Never be frightened to deal with problems - they are part of life.

As consumers we are always looking for a great customer experience. If we don't get it, we will move on to someone else who can give us that experience. This is where, as a business owner, we need to be clear in who we are working with as suppliers and members of our team. They will be 'our' representatives and how they operate can also negatively affect our customer's experience. Anyone we choose to partner with must be able to do what they say they are going to do. They must be able to deliver, so always check the credentials of any person or company you are looking to outsource to.

Think about the customer at all times. They employed your services because they wanted a great customer experience. It is your responsibility to make sure you offer this to them as you may not get a second chance. Get it right the first time.

A note of caution here, though: Don't tell your customer that you over-deliver - just do it. That way, not only are you managing their expectations into your 'standard' timescale, you will also exceed their expectations which reduces the pressure on yourself.

If you happen to be able to over-deliver that is a great service. Always do what you say you are going to do and always offer a great service, but the day you over-promise and under-deliver, is the day you have a problem.

~ ~ ~ ~

70

WHAT HAVE WE LEARNED FROM SITUATIONS OUTSIDE OUR CONTROL?

"Learn from yesterday, live for today, hope for tomorrow. The important thing is to not stop questioning."
~ Albert Einstein

We have to learn from the challenges and experiences of our past and these are things we will constantly face on the journey of running our own businesses. If we don't learn we will without doubt make the same mistake again and again.

Someone once said to me: "We should never fail with the same excuse twice".

We learn more from the failures we make and the challenges we encounter than we ever do from successes. But it is far deeper than this. Obstacles are put in our way to test our mettle, and to see *if* and *how* we overcome them. We will all have come across people who cannot handle these obstacles, instead using them as an excuse to give up on their dream. Yet I firmly believe that if your dream is big enough you will find a way through.

Lets look at a few of these challenges/obstacles:

<u>FINANCIAL</u>

One of the first things to do is to make sure you have a "slush" fund of at least 3 months running costs. This will allow our business to keep functioning if there is an obstacle that cannot be resolved quickly like a recession or a health crisis. We should also review our overheads on at least a quarterly basis to make sure that we are not overspending. We need to make sure we know the financials and the "numbers" relating to our business at ANY given time.

<u>SALES</u>

Sales are what makes our business tick. No matter what our business is, we need to sell something to derive income so we need to keep checking our client base and the profits derived from each client. We may find there are certain sectors in which we are profiting more than others which will help us to maximise our time, effort and spend and use it in the best places for our business. We should also regularly check costs from our suppliers to see if these can be trimmed to reduce our cost of sales. There may be other suppliers who can provide us with the same outcome for less.

CLIENT BASE

Our client base should be kept regularly under review as this will inevitably change over the years of running our business. It may be that we start off working with one type of client and then pick up a client in a different sector which is actually a better fit and more profitable for us. Don't be frightened to evolve or focus more strongly on the most profitable areas of the business. Building strong relationships with your clients is a must.

RELATIONSHIPS

All relationships, not just clients, are vital to the success of our business so we need to make sure that these are strong. This includes everyone we do business with - staff, client or supplier - and everyone that we outsource to. One thing that is paramount is the health and well-being of our staff. Our business will function so much better and be much more effective if we have staff who feel valued, trusted and appreciated. This will also save us time and money. Looking for new staff is an expensive and time-consuming process, so it is far better to really look after the staff that we already have. On top of this, existing and experienced staff will have started to build their own relationships with others in our business which will also go on to yield its own rewards.

Having a quality team is vital to the success of a business:

- We need great staff.
- We need great clients who value the product or service we supply to them and who pay us on time.
- We need great suppliers who can offer us a great service at a great price.
- We need great businesses we can outsource to – Accountants, IT support, HR support, Mentors or Coaches and many others.

If we can address and overcome all of these challenges and obstacles, and ensure we have the right team in place, a successful business will be much easier to achieve.

~ ~ ~ ~

~ 71 ~

ARE YOU TOP OF MIND?

"Top of mind means tip of tongue."
~ Jonah Berger

- Are you at the forefront of your client's minds?

- If they are looking for the service or product that you provide, are you their first port of call?

If you answered *'no'* or *'don't know'* to either or both questions then I'm here to tell you that you should be answering unequivocally, *'yes'*!

I remember when I was running my Ad Agency, I came across many suppliers who wanted to meet me and do business with me, yet these suppliers all offered the same or similar services as each other. I already had contacts I worked with for these services, so the challenge was to discover if I should switch to their offering or remain with the suppliers I had used for years and had a great relationship with.

Initially, most people will use cost as a metric to decide, however it is my experience that you definitely get what you pay for, so I would encourage you to be wary of changing supplier just because you are offered a cheaper service.

The same can be said of service level, so the question I needed to ask was this:

What would it *actually* take for me to change suppliers?

With this in mind, I would have a conversation with all the new prospects, which went something along the lines of this:

"Look, I have been in this business for X number of years. I have built solid relationships with everyone I do business with. I have no need to not do business with them. So if you want to stand a chance of doing business with me, you have to get to know me and I have got to get to know you. The more I hear from you or see you and the more in depth our relationship becomes, the more likelihood there is of me giving you a try, so keep in touch - regularly".

Simple, right? I didn't shut them down. I didn't barter with them on price. All I did was to explain where I was with my business and offered them the chance to show me how they could better what I already had in place.

So, how many of those new providers kept in touch?

Probably less than 10%, which means that at least 90% of them never stood a chance of doing business with me.

For the 10% who did keep in touch, we met on a regular basis and they took the time to get to know me and my business on a deeper level and understand exactly what it was that I needed.

More often than not I would give this 10% the opportunity to supply an element of my business which usually led to more business being passed and a long-term positive relationship.

The point is this: *You have to get to know people. It's never just about business.*

Build those relationships. They will take time, but it's an investment. If you are not prepared to make that investment, then perhaps being a business owner is not the right choice for you.

~ ~ ~ ~

5 Section Five

Growing Your Business

72. NETWORKING - WHY IS IT IMPORTANT TO A SMALL BUSINESS?
73. ARE YOU BUILDING A WIN/WIN BUSINESS?
74. ARE YOU FUTURE PROOFING YOUR INCOME?
75. BUILDING A SUCCESSFUL BUSINESS - WHERE DOES IT START?
76. DO YOU KNOW YOUR TARGET MARKET?
77. DOES YOUR BUSINESS APPEAR TO BE GOING BACKWARDS?
78. NEGATIVE OR POSITIVE MINDSET?
79. STUFF DOESN'T JUST HAPPEN
80. WHAT ARE YOU FRIGHTENED OF?
81. ADVERSITY ~ WHAT CAN WE LEARN?

~ 72 ~

NETWORKING ~ WHY IS IT IMPORTANT TO A SMALL BUSINESS?

"What makes networking work is that it sets up win-win situations
in which all parties involved get to take something home."
~ Earl G. Graves, Sr.

Having owned and run businesses for over 40 years, I always find it difficult when people come to a networking event and tell me it's their first time. Especially if they are an older business owner. I almost want to ask if they have been hiding under a rock.

As you may have gathered, I firmly believe in networking and, if it is done right, it forms a vital part of '*working on*' your business which is something every small business owner should do.

But, what does '**done right**' actually mean?

To begin with, you need to understand what the **main aim of networking** is, which is to **build relationships**. If you have never been networking before or struggle to talk to people then try to resist the urge to give out (or collect) as many business cards as possible rather than striking up a conversation. Doing this or 'working the room', is the fastest way to alienate other attendees.

Building relationships takes time. People need to get to know you and you need to get to know them. It is not an overnight thing so don't expect to understand what someone does based on their 60 second pitch. You need to arrange a one-hour follow up meeting with them which allows each of you thirty minutes to expand on what you do. It is this - what happens outside of the networking meeting - that really counts. This is where relationships are built.

Why is networking so important to small businesses in particular, though?

Simply put, most small businesses are started by people who have never run a business before which means they don't really know how to run a business. They need help and, attending networking events, is the best way to meet those who can help and support them.

It's true when we say that we 'don't know what we don't know' and in the same vein, we 'don't know who we don't know'. Both of these can be overcome by finding external support from others attending networking and similar events.

Before attending, think about the areas of your business that are not your natural strengths and, as a starting point, make sure to book a meeting with someone who can help you with those areas. It is vital that every business owner understands what they are good at and what they are not good at because this, in my experience, is what dictates the businesses which succeed.

What I would say to anyone new to networking is don't join the first networking group you go to. Don't be pressurised. Go to as many networking events as you can on a 'pay as you go' basis. Get a feel for the groups and get a feel for the other attendees. There are a lot of networking groups in most areas so take your time before you make a decision. It will be worth it.

The most important thing is that you need to feel comfortable. If you have never done a 60 second pitch, make sure you prepare it and rehearse it. Take the time to sharpen it so that you can get as much information across as possible. This will also help with any initial nerves. Remember, everyone in the room was new at some point in time.

Remember: the goal of networking is to build relationships. Don't expect to get business from day one. It will take time, so don't get frustrated. People need to get to know you and understand what you do. They want to learn how they can help you as well as how you can support them or others they know.

The process takes time but it is totally worth it.

~ ~ ~ ~

~ 73 ~

ARE YOU BUILDING A WIN-WIN BUSINESS?

"Win-win is a belief in the Third Alternative. It's not your way or my way; it's a better way, a higher way."
~ Stephen Covey

As Stephen Covey says, creating a 'win-win business' is the 'better way'.

When we talk about 'win-win' what we're referring to is the practice of collaborating with another individual or organisation for mutual benefit. At its core, collaboration involves two or more parties working together to achieve a common goal. By entertaining the concept of collaboration in your business, you can provide a massive benefit to the end client.

You'll see from some of my other articles that I talk extensively about how we cannot be all things to all people, and creating a 'win-win' scenario is the perfect example of this. We have to learn not to be all things to all people, and instead, focus on what is in the clients best interests, which often leads to collaboration.

Back in 1990, when I first started networking, I remember passing a lead to someone who, as a result, achieved a £20,000 order for a conservatory. A lot of money today, but even more 30 years ago! I was pleased I'd been able to help link the client to my networking contact, however, when the following week he presented me with a 'cheap' bottle of wine to say thank you, I remember feeling a bit aggrieved. Don't get me wrong, I didn't pass the lead for financial gain, but the difference in outcome for us both, was huge.

There is a phrase used in networking known as *'givers gain'*. This means that if I give business to you, you will give business back to me which sounds really simple, but it often doesn't work. Some people are better at passing referrals than others so, following on from the outcome disparity of the conservatory referral, I realised that it has to be win-win, or there is no longevity in it. From there on I ran my business with that same ethos right up to the day I sold it, and I still like to create win- win situations today, and I teach it to others as well.

Collaboration is a form of win-win. When two people or businesses work together, even if they share the same sector, doing what is right for the client is what counts.

Working in a collaborative mindset helps us all, remember:

"A rising tide raises all ships."

That's exactly what we need to create and when we are going through tough times we can all help each other when we are thinking that way.

When thinking about trying not to be all things to all people, it's helpful to consider those you know who may have more experience in one particular area of client need than you. Recommending your other business contact to your client and saying that whilst you can help them with their need, the person you are referring them to has more experience, undoubtedly gives your client more value.

The bottom line is this:

*Don't think about lining your own pocket above doing
what is right for your client.*

Working in this way and with other business owners with the same mindset will ensure business flows back to you. When I was running my advertising agency, I had a number of business contacts who regularly passed me leads because I would pay them commission for each lead. I paid this commission every time because I recognised that without the input of this business contact, I would not have secured the business in the first place. The commission I paid was agreed between us and regularly reviewed to ensure that neither of us felt our business relationship was imbalanced.

If you run a business in the right way, the better way, you will always win long term. As Stephen Covey says, go with the third alternative.

~ ~ ~ ~

~ 74 ~

ARE YOU FUTURE PROOFING YOUR INCOME?

"The moment you make passive income and portfolio income a part of your life, your life will change. Those words will become flesh."
~ Robert Kiyosaki

Back in 1982, I was fortunate enough to be shown how to create passive income which is something, in my opinion, that we should all do.

Today, most of us find ourselves controlled by our jobs or businesses to the extent that 'they own us' rather than the other way around. This means that if our businesses fail or we lose our job, the income dries up. We should, therefore, never be reliant on just one income. **We should have both an active income (which will be our one and only active income) and we should also have a passive income (which can come from multiple endeavours).**

The quote at the head of this article comes from Robert Kiyosaki who I was fortunate to be able to meet some years ago. I highly recommend his books, in particular, *'Rich Dad, Poor Dad'*.

When the COVID-19 pandemic hit, it proved to be a great leveller for businesses. There were some who faltered and others who seized the opportunity and rose to heights they probably never thought possible. These business were able to create new opportunities out of a bad situation, which is something we all need to learn from. We might not experience another pandemic anytime soon, but recessions are cyclical and come around approximately ever 10 years, so we need to teach ourselves to be the business that succeeds in the face of adversity, not the one that falters.

There are a number of businesses who struggle through recession after recession and learn nothing from them; they are effectively one recession away from going out of business. None of us want to be in that situation which is why passive income is so crucial to our survival. I believe that it is imperative for people to have more than one string to their bow when it comes to income source.

I always had a number of income streams through my business life, and still do today which removes a lot of financial pressure. I guess the question is, how do we generate this passive income?

Well, the good news is that there are so many ways to do this today, so it's worth taking a moment to do some research. Check out what is about both within and outside of your industry, talk to other business owners and find out what they do to generate additional income alongside their active stream, and formulate a plan now. Don't wait for the next recession.

Also, don't worry about what others say. They do not pay your bills, yet are always happy to stick their oar in and tell you why you shouldn't do this or why you should do that. As I have said before in previous articles, many of us are in this bubble of mediocrity; your friends want to see you succeed **as long as** you don't succeed more than them.

If your business is doing well, this is no reason to ignore the potential of passive income. None of us know what is around the corner and a business doing well can disappear in a very short period of time if income dries up. *It is better to be safe than sorry,* which was a phrase used often by previous generations. One that I hardly seem to hear today, yet it remains so true.

If your business is doing well, great. If you are earning enough from your business, fantastic, but, if you add to that and develop other streams of income then you open up things like the possibility of early retirement. Or you can have a luxury holiday every year. Whatever your goal, it will be achieved more readily if you future proof your income and develop some streams of passive income.

Bear in mind, in order for passive income to work, you will need to spend some time initially 'kicking it off' - developing a training course, for example - but your initial time investment will be repaid by ongoing passive income once it is up and running. If you have spare capacity in your office, you could think about renting it out, or creating a 'hub' or co-working area. If you're into the housing market, then buying a property to rent out is a great way to generate passive income. As long as you charge more rent than your mortgage or loan repayment, you will be receiving additional income each month.

There are so many opportunities out there.

Think passive income. Don't become a business which falters at the first hurdle.

~ ~ ~ ~

75

BUILDING A SUCCESSFUL BUSINESS ~ WHERE DOES IT START?

*"You gotta have a dream, if you don't have a dream, how you gonna
make a dream come true?"*
~ Oscar Hammerstein II

I'm sure you've heard this quote many times, though perhaps normally attributed it to a Walt Disney film, however it is a great quote to bear in mind when it comes to business.

So, let's begin by looking at what a dream is and how it differs from a goal.

Dreams are something we think about, often to the extent that they dominate our thoughts, and it is our dreams that drive us to do things. *Goals*, then, are the action of the dream. Without action, goals cannot be achieved and they will remain simply a dream.

In the same way, if we don't apply action to our dreams, then they will remain a *fantasy* - something you constantly think about but will probably never achieve.

Everything starts with a dream and I believe that we should all dream big. Having a dream helps to make the impossible, possible. According to Richard Branson, we should '*all take time out regularly just to dream*'.

Too many of us get weighed down in *doing*, and forget to take the time to *think* and *feel* - and *dream*. If we do allow ourselves to dream, though, it's important to remember that if they *don't scare us, they are probably too small*. Dreams - certainly when it comes to business - should be something that stretch us.

Any of us who have started a business would have started with a dream. The problem is that once our business gets underway and we start facing challenges, we lose sight of the dream. The dream, though, should always be in our mind as without it, why are we doing what we do? Whatever your dream is, put a picture where you see it every day – on the fridge is a good place, especially if you – like me – are always going there.

In order for us to achieve our dreams, we need to put action in, which means setting goals to keep us on track. We should also continually monitor ourselves to make sure we stay on track and a great way to do this is to associate with successful and like-minded people and/or read personal/business development books. I personally think business books are great because they help us not only with business ideas, they are also incredibly motivational and inspirational and will help us to take focused.

Having a *big dream* should be our main focus, broken up into 'stepping stones' of goals. When we achieve each 'stepping stone' goal, we need to reward ourselves and recognise that we are one step closer to realising our big dream.

When it comes to the reward, it should be in line with the goal. Don't, for example, go and spend £500 on your reward when the goal was to make £50 more profit. Flip it on its head and instead wait until you've made £500 in profit before you spend £50 on your reward. That way your bottom line will not be negatively impacted.

Whatever you choose to do, though, make sure you celebrate your achievement - it's a great way to keep your motivation high as you make your way towards the next stepping stone.

~ ~ ~ ~

76

DO YOU KNOW YOUR TARGET MARKET?

"Stopping advertising to save money is like stopping your watch to save time."
~ Henry Ford

As an advertising specialist, it is only fitting that I include at least one article on how to get the most from your advertising. A quote from David Ogilvy sums up the purpose of advertising:

"If it doesn't sell, it isn't creative."

Meaning, if our advertising is not resulting in sales, we need to be creative with our advertising message, regardless of where it appears. Whether it be on a billboard, a website, on social media or promoting ourselves at a networking event we need to make sure that our advertising is creative.

To begin, we need an attention grabbing headline - this is the only way your audience will read on. It needs to be big and bold, therefore, and take up somewhere near to a third of the advertising space. You then need to put your contact details at the bottom of the advert.

The key to advertising is to remember that no one cares what your name is. All they care about is how you can help them. You could then, pose a question that is relative to your target market, but it needs to be powerful. You need to understand that however you are advertising, the only people who are going to be interested in the product or service you are selling are those who are looking for that product or service at that particular time. This is why you need a really powerful message.

I networked with other business owners for over 30 years and often heard the same message over and again causing me, and many others to switch off. That's never going to be good for sales. What you need to do in all of your advertising endeavours is to change the message regularly and make it powerful.

If you are delivering a networking pitch, start with an attention grabbing headline or statement or question that most - if not all - the people in the room will relate to. You can end the pitch with your name and business name and contact details, but the main thing is treat your 60 second pitch as an advertising opportunity and make it creative. If you know your target market, then make sure the message is aimed at this market and not aimed at everyone who hears or reads your advertising message. Narrow it down. If your target market at a networking event is - for example - accountants, then mention this to everyone in the room. Not only will they be clear on whether or not they can help you, they will also be clear on who they might know that they can refer to you.

Another good way to make your presentation creative and interesting is to talk about what you have done over the last week, or maybe a particular conversation you had - anything that the others in the room will be able to relate to.

If we want to be successful, we all need to think harder about our messages and be realistic about the responses we are receiving. If these are not our desired outcome then it isn't because 'networking doesn't work', it's more likely due to our message being off or unclear.

We also need to think about what we are saying and to whom and accept that the outcome, whether that be positive or negative, relies on us. If we choose to stop advertising our business in any format, especially if we are doing it to save money, we are going to essentially be on a fool's errand. As Henry Ford so eloquently states at the head of this article, 'stopping advertising to save money is like stopping your watch to save time.'

Advertising - in any format - works. The response is purely based on how creative the message is so make sure you bear this in mind next time you do a networking pitch or post an advertisement. Make sure you stand out from the crowd and avoid recycling the same message. That is a guaranteed way to lose the attention of your audience and you want to grab and retain their attention for as long as you possibly can.

~ ~ ~ ~

77

DOES YOUR BUSINESS APPEAR TO BE GOING BACKWARDS?

"Don't dwell on what went wrong. Instead, focus on what to do next.
Spend your energies on moving forward toward finding the answer."
~ Denis Waitley.

I was speaking to a good friend and business colleague recently, and we were talking about the highs and lows of being in business. Every business owner will have their fair share of highs and lows - though we hope that there are more highs than lows - and, if we run our business the right way, then there is no reason why there shouldn't be more highs. If you're experiencing more lows, then perhaps there are things that you should consider changing.

You need to make sure you always end each day on a high. Finishing on a low and starting the next day with that same low in your mind will not set you up right. Finish on a high and the next day will start on a high, however, if your business still seems to be going backwards, think of this analogy:

An arrow can only be shot by pulling it backward. When business and life
is dragging you back with difficulties, it means it's going to launch you into
something great. So just focus and keep aiming.

Maintaining focus is vital for success, as is having a positive attitude. You need to focus with the end goal in mind and cannot allow anything to detract from this goal.

When I ran the London Marathon for the first time in 2004 at the of age 47, I trained to complete it and there was no way I was not going to finish. My focus through the whole 12 months training up to the day of the event was on my friends who were running with me along with the people who had sponsored me and the Charity we were running for. On all of my training runs, I made sure to run with the right attitude so that I gave myself every chance of finishing.

We all go through our regular dose of crap in business and life and it is important to remember it is not **what happens to us**, but **how we react to it**. We must react positively and maintaining focus helps us to do this.

When we go through tough times in life and in business, this is when we really need to be creative and think of different ways of doing what we are doing or expand our offerings.

Putting processes in place to help us not only get through this issue, but to come out stronger once we are through it, is so important here. The new processes we put in place should then be something we keep on board as an extra service. Don't just do it for the short term, always be thinking long term.

Challenges from external circumstances are always going to be there but, if we allow them to control us and we sit and do nothing, then we may not get through those hard times. What we need to do is prepare ourselves with a solution we can use in the future. It's no good thinking about the 'what ifs', because they will always invariably become the 'what wills'.

It is also vital to make sure we surround ourselves with positive, upbeat people and not people who are going to constantly try and drag us down. Association with the right people will have a massive impact on the success of our business and will also help us maintain the focus.

Use each day, week and month wisely. Stay positive and recognise that there are going to be times when it won't be easy, but keep a look out for opportunities. Those who find the most creative solutions will come through any and all challenges as a much stronger business (and person) than they were before the storm.

~ ~ ~ ~

78

NEGATIVE OR POSITIVE MINDSET?

"A positive attitude gives you power over your circumstances instead of your circumstances having power over you."
~ Joyce Meyer

Do you believe you have a negative mindset? Are you affected by external circumstances? Do you let others control your attitude?

Hopefully, you answered all of these questions with an emphatic, NO!

Yet, as much as we might like to think we are positive all of the time, and that we don't let external circumstances or people control our attitudes, we have to be honest and admit that we slip from time to time. Maintaining a positive attitude can be exhausting so when we do slip, it's important to make sure it is not at a critical time, for example in a one-to-one meeting, or when we are in the office with our team, or when we are hosting an event, or appearing on a Zoom call.

My best advice is to make sure that any slips towards the negative, occur in the privacy of your own home and preferably not at the same time as those you live with. If you're all feeling negative it will be much harder to pull through, so the key is to have someone you can confide in and let them know you are struggling and need help.

As the quote says, *when we have a positive attitude, it gives us power over our circumstances*, and that's because *when we think positively, we act positively.*

That's why I always advise business owners to hang around those who are giving off positive vibes. Their vibe will rub off on us which is important, not only for ourselves but also for those we come into contact with. We want people to feel *better when we walk into a room*, not *relieved when we leave that room.*

Bear in mind though, even people who appear positive all the time will have their moments of doubt. The difference is often that they are better at hiding negative feelings or concerns. Remember, we can all sound confident yet feel anxious inside. We can look healthy, yet feel awful. We can look happy but feel miserable. We can look good and still feel ugly.

The message here is one of kindness. We need to learn to be kind because every person can, or almost certainly is, fighting a battle we know nothing about. We all need help from time to time and we shouldn't be frightened to ask for it.

This is why it is crucial we surround ourselves with positive upbeat people. When we are feeling low, being around the right people can raise our mood. The following quote is a great illustration of this:

> *"You will be the same person in five years as you are today except for the people you meet and the books you read."*
>
> *— Charlie Tremendous Jones*

When we are in a positive mindset, we spot opportunities - not just for ourselves, but for others, too. These opportunities are always there but if we don't have a positive mindset, we will not spot them. When we acknowledge that every opportunity we miss represents an opportunity for our competitors, we can see how important it is to maintain a positive mindset as much as possible.

Keeping an 'inner circle' of people whose thoughts are aligned with ours is a great way to ensure we don't miss out.

~ ~ ~ ~

79

STUFF DOESN'T JUST HAPPEN

"Most of the time, stuff doesn't just happen TO us - we MAKE it happen
by what we do and the way we are."
~ Tony Jeary

Stuff doesn't just happen.

Over the years, so many times I have heard comments along the lines of:

"I went out of business because of the recession."

"The financial crash ruined my business."

"It's the government's fault I went out of business."

There are countless '*excuses*' or '*justifiable reasons*' as to why someone had to close the doors of their business, along with explanations as to why their dream has gone up in smoke, but how many people do you think point the finger of blame squarely at themselves?

In my opinion, not enough. I firmly believe that businesses fail more often than not due to the activities (or inactivity) of those at the helm. Of course, there are external contributors, but is it too easy to simply blame these external factors rather than looking within ourselves?

We must accept responsibility for our actions. The one person we are totally in control of is ourselves. External stuff happens but we need to understand that we have no control over this; what we do have control over, though, is how we react.

Generally, when business owners cease trading, it's possible to identify an underlying issue that has been bubbling for months or years. If the business owner has chosen to ignore it or has tried to work their way through it without asking for help and/or support, this is where they often come unstuck.

During my time in business I weathered many issues including two recessions, a depression and the dissolution of a business partnership. I built my business from scratch and was able to sell it as an ongoing successful venture because I knew the importance of being creative, of reinventing myself.

We have to be aware of what the economy or market is doing, and react accordingly, crucially, before it's too late. We need to be proactive and make sure we spend time working ON our business as well as the daily activities required to work IN our business.

The key for me was understanding what I was good at and getting help for the things I was not good at. We, as the business owner, can be too close to the action meaning we don't always spot the signs of a problem. Bringing in external support can help identify these, hopefully before they become a risk to the survival of our business.

Also, we are can be very blinkered when it comes to making decisions about our own business. Somebody who has run a business for years, though, will have undoubtedly experienced the challenges we are experiencing and can help guide us through these to a positive resolution.

In business, there will always be the *'what ifs'*. *'What if'* this happens, *'what if'* that happens - concerns which could stop us in our tracks. Preparing our businesses to handle anything that is thrown at it will help greatly when we encounter those 'what ifs'. Why? Because we will have a plan to overcome them. If we don't have a plan and we don't know what to do, we stand a chance of wallowing in our own self-pity and allowing the situation to swallow us up.

When I say that 'stuff doesn't just happen', what I mean is that if we know our business has potential issues, we have to address them, not ignore them, and we have to address them NOW. We must always be in total control of our business which sometimes means asking for help rather than thinking we can solve every problem ourselves.

We cannot assume that because we have always done things a certain way, we should continue to do them that way. If it isn't working then it is pointless to keep doing it. If we make no changes, nothing will change which is pretty much the *definition of insanity doing the same thing day after day and expecting a different outcome*

It can be difficult if you are the sort of person who doesn't like change, but in order to run a successful business it is imperative to be aware of and embrace this change. Remember, change will often happen and may well be outside of our control, but what we can control is how we react to it.

~ ~ ~ ~

~ 80 ~

WHAT ARE YOU FRIGHTENED OF?

"I learned that courage was not the absence of fear, but the triumph over it. The brave man is not he who does not feel afraid, but he who conquers that fear."
~ Nelson Mandela

When I originally wrote this article it was in the midst of the global pandemic and we were definitely living through the strangest of times. We all became fearful of so many things such as going out in public, being in crowds, meeting anyone face to face and, ultimately, the fear of dying.

As humans, fear is natural, but what I realised as a result of the pandemic was that I (and by extension, you) need to be careful of what we fear because fear can be all consuming to the extent we are unable to think or react rationally. It doesn't take long for this to become a negative cycle and before we know it, we end up doing nothing except sitting and thinking about our entire lives - in a negative way.

FEAR stops us doing so many things. In my years of being in business I have come across many fears, both fears that I held but also the fears of others. Some common examples are:

! Fear of public speaking
! Fear of having a conversation with a difficult client.
! Fear of presenting a 60-second networking pitch.
! Fear of making a phone call.
! Fear of solving a problem.
! Fear of failure.
! Fear of success.

FEAR will stop us moving forward. If we want to move forward we have to overcome our fears and in my experience there is nothing like just doing it. Facing that fear. Once you have done it - from that moment forward - it becomes easier. It may well continue to be uncomfortable for a while, but it will get easier, so the sooner you face that fear, the better.

Fear can also be a factor in keeping us stuck in something I refer to as the *'bubble of mediocrity'*.

This bubble happens when our friends and families support us and **want us to succeed,** but **they don't want us to succeed more than them.** Their intentions may be coming from a place of 'protection', wanting to protect us from the unknown, which they achieve by feeding our fears and holding us back.

Most of the population are in this *'bubble of mediocrity'*, often because there is safety in numbers. It takes enormous strength to move outside this bubble; for every person who tries to pull away, there are several people trying to hold us back. When we do manage to step outside the bubble, it could mean leaving others behind, people we may have known for years.

When this happens, the key is to build new relationships with people who think like us. Doing this takes great inner strength and faith in ourselves because it can be difficult to maintain the belief that we are doing the right thing. The pull to drag us back into this bubble can be so powerful that the only way to maintain our strength of belief is to surround ourselves with those who tell us that, 'we can do it', that they will 'help us' and that they have 'belief in us'.

It is understandable why stepping outside this bubble is frightening - we are leaving behind things we have always known - however anyone who has stepped outside this bubble will tell you that it's actually not scary at all. In reality, there are more people willing to help us succeed and overcome our fears than there are keeping us inside the bubble. These people will go on to become strong, lifetime friends, they will take us under their wing and introduce us to others who can support us and add value to our businesses and lives.

Sometimes others believe in us long before we believe in ourselves but, if we have the courage of our convictions and do what we believe is right, we can achieve success regardless of whether others agree and approve or not.

~ ~ ~ ~

ADVERSITY ~ WHAT CAN WE LEARN?

"It is your reaction to adversity, not the adversity itself that determines how your life's story will develop."
~ Dieter F Uchtdorf

As the quote above says, it is how we react to adversity and what we learn from it that will determine our life's story.

I am thankful to my IT support company - **Magikos IT** and **Tony Donoghue** in particular - for convincing me to move all my business data to the cloud 10 years ago as this enabled me and my team to be able to pick up laptops and go home the moment the government announced that we needed to work from home due to the worldwide pandemic back in 2020. There were no ands, ifs or buts as we were all set up to be able to work from home. Many businesses, sadly, did not have such measures in place which meant they struggled with the adversity which the onset of the pandemic brought.

Bearing this in mind, I thought it would be helpful to summarise some advice I have found helpful when faced with business adversity:

TIP 1 - Plan Well in Advance and use Expert Advice

We have to know what we are good at and focus on that skill and outsource everything else. Our outsourced suppliers will have to look after their own businesses and if you have chosen those suppliers wisely, they will give you advance notice of anything on the horizon that could impact your business. In the same way, you should be able to keep your clients/customers in the loop regarding the industry you are in. We cannot be all things to all people and asking for help and getting expert advice is a strength, not a weakness.

TIP 2 - Go Networking: It will Really Help Your Business

Networking with other business owners is a great way to keep informed and updated on issues that could impact our business. They are an environment to learn from others and keep connected. These are important reasons to go networking, more important in my book than looking for clients or people who will spend money on the services we offer. Networking is about building relationships, not selling your product or service. This will happen if you focus on those relationships first.

TIP 3 - Build strong relationships ~ Put people front and centre of all decisions.

When I first started my business, I was taught not to worry about making money and to focus, instead, on building relationships. The advice concluded that if I had a product or service which was in demand, the sales would come - advice that was spot on. I have so many people to thank over the years who I have been fortunate enough to build relationships with. They have all given me invaluable advice and support; from Brian Smith, my business mentor to Mary Flavelle, my networking mentor, there have been literally hundreds of people who have helped me along the way. I know that without putting those relationships first and front and centre, I would never have achieved the levels of success that I did.

TIP 4 - Don't Try and be All Things to all People ~ Ask for Help

Following on from TIP 1, it is vital to not try to be all things to all people. You cannot do it. Running a business is not about doing everything. Yes, it will cost money to employ an HR Consultant, IT support, Bookkeeper, Accountant and so on, but look at this as an investment in your business, not a cost. Remember, other than an accountant, you are paying for the hours you need those outsourced services. It is important to understand the benefits of outsourced support. Don't, for example, wait for your laptop to crash before you do something about it. Don't try to fix it yourself. It will only cost your more in the long run.

TIP 5 - Attend a Personal Development Programme

Personal development is vital to success - in my opinion. Reading a personal development book on a monthly basis (or listening to an audio book) will have an amazing impact on you as a person. Your attitude will change for the better. Your relationships will change for the better. You will be more confident. Building ourselves as well as building our businesses can happen at networking events, seminars we attend, presentations we listen to, TED talks, conversations over coffee, etc. The books we read and the work we do on our personal development we shape our future self.

Finally and to show entrepreneurship in the UK is alive and well, I found this comment:

"According to analysis by the Centre for Entrepreneurs, nearly half a million companies were launched in the UK between March and September this year, an increase of 44,500 compared to the same period in 2019".

We are strong in this country, we do believe in ourselves. All I would ask is for more businesses to ask for help and stop trying to do anything themselves.

~ ~ ~ ~

6 Section Six

Being Business Savvy

82. DON'T BUY THINGS YOU CAN'T AFFORD
83. DON'T BUILD YOUR CASTLE IN SOMEONE ELSE'S GARDEN
84. DO YOU REALLY UNDERSTAND NETWORKING?
85. HOW GOOD ARE YOU AT DUE DILIGENCE?
86. HOW GOOD ARE YOU AT SPOTTING OPPORTUNITIES?
87. HOW NETWORKING CAN SAVE (& MAKE) YOU THOUSANDS OF POUNDS
88. THE POWER OF EFFECTIVE COMMUNICATION
89. WHY, ONLY WHEN IT REALLY HURTS, DO SO MANY TAKE ACTION?
90. CHANGE ~ ARE OUR BUSINESSES SET UP TO COPE?

82

DON'T BUY THINGS YOU CAN'T AFFORD
(to impress people you don't know or don't like)

"I always say if you can't buy it three times over, you can't afford it.
Don't drive a Bentley on a Benz income."
~ Slim Thug

We all have to learn from our own experiences or those whose advice we trust, but there is nothing like experiencing it yourself.

Very early on in my business life, I went to visit a prospective client and was immediately impressed with the cars they drove, the office they had and the fact they seemed to be doing really well. I mentioned this to one of my trusted advisers and he told me not to be fooled by material possessions. He said it is very easy for people to make it look like they are doing better than they really are. He then went on to say that it was unlikely that this prospective client owned the cars or the office, rather that they would be on finance. It turned out he was correct. Less than two years later, said prospect had gone out of business due to over committing themselves.

We are all guilty of this to a degree. It is very easy, once we have a bit of cash in our hands or win a new piece of business, to spend it on *something we want* but *don't necessarily need*, which can sometimes lead to financial danger.

Here, then, are six financial tips, all of which I've taken from personal experience:

1. Never take out of the business more than you need to ensure you can keep a roof over your head and support you and your family. Your business has to be looked at as one of your family members, so look after this in the same way as you look after your family. Don't rob Peter to pay Paul.

2. As regards the vehicle you drive, don't overspend. If you are building a business, you need to enjoy the fruits of your labour but it doesn't make sense to financially commit to a vehicle on a three or four year lease based purely on one piece of business you won the day before. If you're going to lease a vehicle, commit to one that you know you will be able to fund for that three to four year period. At the end of the day whatever vehicle you buy, you only need it to get you from A to B.

3. Constantly keep an eye on your business costs. Check them on a quarterly basis to make sure you are not spending more money than you need. All business expenditure should be checked and it's worth remembering that sometimes it's easier to reduce costs than it is to increase income. When you start networking you will find people who can supply every service you are ever likely to need, but you need to exercise caution in which of those you use. If you have too many 'suppliers' then you might end up running your business just to fund these suppliers, which doesn't make financial sense.

4. Know what your financial liabilities are going to be well in advance of when they are due. Don't spend money that is not rightfully yours - by this I mean money that you have set aside to cover tax or VAT or rent, for example. You cannot and must not use the excuse that you don't have the money to pay these expenses. Ignorance is not an excuse.

5. Make sure you prepare for the 'what ifs'. We may not know what these are likely to be, but we do know recessions happen approximately once every ten years, for example, so we can implement a long-term plan in this respect.

6. Business does not stand still and if we are doing the same thing this year as we were doing last year, we are probably going backwards. We need to make sure we have a "slush fund" to cover situations like this as well as making sure we are constantly reinventing ourselves rather than living on past successes. We must always be looking to the future.

Running a business is fun. Hopefully there will be more ups than downs, but don't try to do everything yourself. Ask for help - this is a strength, not a weakness.

And, most importantly:

Think carefully before you spend your hard-earned income.
Do not act on impulse and regret it later.

~ ~ ~ ~

83

DON'T BUILD YOUR CASTLE IN SOMEONE ELSE'S GARDEN

"Yes, your home is your castle, but it is also your identity and your possibility to be open to others."
~ David Soul

We have all heard the quote that *our home is our castle*, but why would we build our castle in someone else's garden?

The title for this piece came from the quote, '*don't build your castle in someone else's garden*', which was given to me by my good friend Tony Donoghue.

What, though, does it mean?

Consider, how many business owners you know who don't have a website. Instead, they rely on their Facebook page or their LinkedIn profile which they utilise as their business hub. In this situation, they are '*building their castle in someone else's garden*' because they don't own or have any control over these platforms. They are having to play by the platform's rules, not their own.

On the face of it, this doesn't sound like too much of an issue, however one wrong word or post or comment and they (Facebook, LinkedIn et al) can delete your account and business page including all testimonials, conversations and contact information. This might sound harsh, but they are perfectly entitled to do this because they own your data, not you. That means everything you have worked hard to build is lost and there is nothing you can do about it. Madness, eh? But this is exactly how some people build their businesses.

I'm not suggesting that you shouldn't have a Facebook or LinkedIn page or other social media presence, but what I am saying is that these should be in addition to building your own website. You should then steer all traffic from these pages to your website because this is **your** space that you own and control.

Your website is yours which means you can do what you want with it. The data collected is yours to use - as long as you have the consent of those whose data you've collected - and you can build as many castles as you like. The only thing I would say if you are a UK based business, is to make sure your website is hosted on a UK server. It's also good to check that you own the content and rights to that site and page and that these are not retained by your web builder. If you don't own these, you need to sort that out as soon as possible. It's never a problem until it becomes a problem!

When you are running a business, make sure you have total control of any intellectual property rights - logos, strapline, website etc. If you are unsure, it might be worth speaking to an IP (Intellectual Property) Lawyer to make sure you are covered and are not inadvertently using a logo or a name that is copyrighted or trademarked by someone else. I would recommend making sure you check this before going too far down the road with setting up your business.

The lesson here is simple:

Your castle, your garden, your rules.

Your castle, someone else's garden, their rules.

It's really worth taking the time to make sure that you and your business are protected. The last thing you want to do is build in someone else's garden and lose all of your hard work.

~ ~ ~ ~

84

DO YOU REALLY UNDERSTAND NETWORKING?

"You can have everything in life you want, if you will just help other people get what they want."
~ Zig Ziglar

Networking at its heart gives us power - the power of association. Yet it still amazes me how few people really understand what networking is about and how effective it can be if we do it right.

As the late, great *Zig Ziglar* said:

"You can have everything in life you want, if you will just help other people get what they want".

In other words, we have to give before we get. It is how life works. We need to take our eyes off ourselves and put them on others. Networking will not work for you if your attitude is to attend events solely to sell your products or services, so if this is what you are doing STOP and STOP NOW! If you meet me at a networking meeting and this is what you do to me, I will delete you. Whatever relationship we could have developed will stop there and then.

I remember years ago, an article by the Thames Valley Chamber of Commerce chronicled *"A Day In The Life Of A Serial Networker."* This article was an insult to those of us who understand how to network. The guy in question never attended any networking event more than once. He worked the networking circuit and every associated room, selling his wares. That guy - in my opinion - is an idiot. How can you ever expect to pick up business if you are not building relationships?

We need to be respectful of others at networking events. If someone asks you what you do - whether on Zoom or face to face - please make sure you give them time to explain what they do and ask how you can help them as well. It has to be a two-way conversation. Remember, true networking is about helping others, looking out for your fellow networkers by trying to connect them to your contacts who might be beneficial.

"Give and you shall receive", is a well-known biblical proverb which stands true today and is so important when it comes to running and growing your business.

I recently arranged a face to face meeting with a new contact and, after the customary introductions and necessary order of coffee, his first question to me was, "What can I help you with?"

Which sounds great, the perfect start. He openly wanted to help me, except, that's not what he meant. He was under the impression I wanted to employ his services and was asking 'what he could help me with' in that context.

The meeting continued, though it was totally one-sided. I was the one asking questions, finding out what he did and discovering who he wished to be introduced to. Not once did he ask what I did and how he could help me with my business. Despite this, I still agreed to promote his services to my LinkedIn connections which I did. I am sure some of them will go on to use his services and whilst I haven't received anything directly in return, I am fine with this.

Why?

Because I know that by me putting his services out there, by helping him, it will be paid back to me one way or another. Not necessarily through this chap or his connections, but it will return in some way which is often from the most unexpected sources. The best way to think about taking action from networking is this:

- Help others by asking open-ended questions.
- Spend time finding out and them, their business and their lives.
- Offer to help them in any way you can.
- Connect them to your contacts.
- Don't worry if you don't get chance to talk about yourself. Many people like to talk about themselves and over the years I have learned to simply let them. It will come back.

Give and you shall receive.

Just have faith.

~ ~ ~ ~

85

HOW GOOD ARE YOU AT DUE DILIGENCE?

"Care and diligence bring luck."
~ Thomas Fuller

Isn't it amazing how, when your mind is open, ideas come?

When chatting to a connection a few years ago, the subject turned to franchises and business, which led us to conclude that not enough care is taken when hiring staff, or finding suppliers to outsource to, or buying a franchise. This care can be summed up in two words:

Due Diligence

Two words that, if done correctly, can make a mountain of difference to your business. If not done correctly, a lack of due diligence can cost thousands of pounds.

In its simplest terms, **due diligence** can be defined as the investigation or exercise of care that a (reasonable) business person would usually be expected to take before entering into any agreement.

Most of us would use it when we are taking on a new member of staff by checking out that person via social media or talking to previous employers or referees. To take someone on as a new member of the team without finding out more about them would be classed as a risky decision. It might work out and yet, it might not which could potentially cause untold damage to our business.

Do we, though, carry out this level of due diligence when taking on a new supplier or outsourced business (such as an HR consultant or business coach)? If we don't do this, how do we know that those businesses are trustworthy? How do we know that they will add value to our business? How do we know they will deliver the service we need and not simply take our money and run?

I've met so many business owners who have 'employed' the services of those they've met at a networking event, without doing any due diligence whatsoever. They are giving that person a basic level of trust, simply because they met at a business networking event - but these stories don't always end happily. Sometimes, without doing any real due diligence, regardless of where we meet people, we can end up getting financially or 'reputation-ally' burned.

We should always check out outsourced suppliers with a great deal of care and attention. Do not rush into a decision and regret it later. It is better to take our time, check them out carefully, maybe have more than one meeting. If they are genuine and wish to work with you and have nothing to hide, then they will understand and will not try to rush you into a decision.

Franchises can also fall foul of the due diligence test. Many franchises are purchased by people who have a sizeable redundancy payout, or who have been left money in an estate, for example. They see a franchise model as an easy way to get into business - and it can be, however there are countless franchise opportunities out there and sadly, not all of them are worth the time, effort and more crucially, the money.

In the course of my work I have met many people who have invested in a franchise business, only to regret it six months later. The most common regret is that, had they looked into it more thoroughly, they would have realised they could have built exactly the same business themselves, without the need for the franchisor who (usually) requires a monthly payment fee. This is a classic example of the importance of due diligence in all areas of business.

Though I have illustrated a situation where simply meeting someone at a networking event does not guarantee they are above board, I still firmly believe that networking is at the heart of every good business. When we dedicate our time to networking - properly - we will build a large database of small business owners who can add value to our business. Over a period of time we will build relationships with these other businesses which is, in and of itself, part of a good due diligence practice. Astonishingly, only 5% of small businesses in the UK actively network, which, in my experience, leaves so many of them completely exposed and open to being taken advantage of.

Not only do we need to do our own due diligence, but we also need to be aware of those around us. If we can, we should always connect others to someone we know who is trustworthy which, at the end of the day, will save them a lot of heartache.

Do your due diligence. It will help you more than you can possibly know.

~ ~ ~ ~

86

HOW GOOD ARE YOU AT SPOTTING OPPORTUNITIES?

"Opportunities are like sunrises. If you wait too long, you miss them."
~ William Arthur Ward

As business owners, we should all spend a good percentage of our time working ON our businesses and looking for new opportunities. We cannot just assume that whatever we have been doing up until now will always produce us an income. Things change and we must change with them or risk getting left behind.

I remember as my Advertising Agency was growing in the early 2000's, there never seemed to be a month go by where a new advertising medium wasn't being introduced to the market. It was difficult to keep on top of it at times but I knew that I had to embrace these opportunities or risk getting left behind.

One day, I was sitting on the train coming back from London and I started to wonder how many opportunities had come to the market in the last couple of years, so I started to write them down. By the time I'd finished I had covered one and a half sides of A4 paper. There were close to 50 opportunities, yet, when I had started in business, there had been only 5. This meant an additional 45 opportunities to present to my clients as advertising solutions. How, I wondered, would I explain these to my clients in simple terms?

In the end I created an A4 PDF with a one inch photo of each opportunity. Below each photo I added two words of explanation which made it easy for clients to see their options. We then attached this PDF to every outgoing email, making sure it reached all of our clients. Welcoming these additional advertising opportunities was part of our business evolution which, had we not embraced it, would have almost certainly affected the business' longevity.

Opportunities are always there, and always have been. If we are not looking for them, we won't notice them. If we are going round with blinkers on or we are not thinking straight, if we have negative things going in on our lives or if we are under stress, we miss these opportunities.

When it comes to business, we need to de-clutter our brains and focus on two things:

1. Doing what we're good at.

2. Spending time working ON our business.

Ideally we should then be outsourcing everything else and stop trying to be all things to all people, otherwise we will never move forward and never be able to move beyond working IN our business.

The pace the business world is changing can be frightening at times, so it's important to keep up to date with the changes in our industries. The way to become a market leader is to recognise and adopt new opportunities before everyone else which means always being on the look out for the next opportunity. We must be constantly evolving, because this is what will keep us in business.

For every company that has evolved and become successful, there are countless others who have failed, largely due to the fact that they didn't see the opportunities that were out there.

Here are some top tips for evolving:

1. We must have an open mind.

2. We must have a clear mind.

3. Our minds are like a parachute - they only work when they are open.

4. We need to ask for help so that we can be a better business.

5. We need to aim to become a market leader by seizing opportunities.

6. Then we must use those opportunities to keep our businesses fresh.

Doing the same thing and expecting a different result is only ever going to have one result - and trust me, it's not the one that you want.

~ ~ ~ ~

87

HOW NETWORKING CAN SAVE (& MAKE) YOU THOUSANDS OF POUNDS

"If you want to go fast, go alone. If you want to go far, go with others."
~ African Proverb

I have never doubted the power of networking to help you build a better business. Networking is key when it comes to building relationships, working collaboratively with others and finding quality outsourced suppliers. It can also save, or make, you thousands of pounds.

When I was running my business I would attend networking events at least five times a week, using networking as part of my business strategy for over 30 years. I was even networking when there was literally only one networking organisation in the UK.

As I've mentioned in earlier articles, networking is NOT about working the room and selling your product or service to everyone there. If you're doing this, please don't. It's only going to annoy the other attendees and will end up damaging your reputation.

Networking is about building strong relationships and looking for people who can add value to your business. Yes, we are all there to promote our own businesses but it is so much easier to get customers and clients if you build relationships and care about others first.

The follow up is the most important part of networking. If you attend one networking event every week - and a lot of people do - you will have heard everyone do their one minute pitch each week which means you will have listened to each attendee speak for 52 minutes over the course of a year. However, the reality is that most pitches are recycled so you've probably only really heard them speak for 1 minute and switched off for the other 51.

How then, can you possible get to know someone like this?

You can't. Which is why you need to follow up after the meeting. Take time to build relationships. Get to know people. You'll be surprised what comes out of follow up meetings. Imagine if the person you're now talking to, personally knows the MD of the company you've been trying to get in front of for years!

I have spoken to many contacts over the years who have bought into franchises and almost without exception, each one has said that if they'd known how many people they could have engaged with through networking, they would never have bought into a franchise. They would have saved themselves thousands of pounds and set up the business on their own.

Pretty much every supplier I used during the time I was running my business was someone I met through networking. Over time I got to know them, maybe met them socially even, and spoke to others who they had worked with. Eventually I reached a level where I knew I could trust them to look after me and my business.

Though 'employing' the services of someone you met at a networking event doesn't always end positively, the fact that you are seeing them on a regular basis and can ask as many questions as you need, will definitely equip you to make the best judgement. And remember, it's not in their interest to give you a bad service because not only will they have let you down, you will also share your experience with the rest of the networking group. The power of 'word of mouth' will do the rest and it won't be long before their reputation is damaged for good.

The FSB (Federation of Small Businesses) have published figures which state there are around 5.5 million businesses in the UK of which 4.5 million are classed as micro businesses - those that employ less than 10 people. If only 5% of all micro businesses are regularly networking, that's still a pool of 225,000 potential contacts. For the remaining 95% who might not currently network, they will be facing an uphill battle to find those they 'know, like and trust' to collaborate with. Networking works and we need to share that message to every small and micro business owner we meet.

Keep networking, keep building those relationships, keep having those 121's. The networking community is very much alive and thriving.

~ ~ ~ ~

~ 88 ~

THE POWER OF EFFECTIVE COMMUNICATION

"The biggest communication problem is we do not listen to understand.
We listen to reply."
~ Stephen R Covey

Good effective communication is one of the most important keys to success.

During a networking meeting a couple of years ago, the attendees were put into a breakout room to discuss a particular topic. The title of the topic was: "How do we convert prospects?"

Each group had a variety of different responses, all of which had one element in common: **relationships.**

Relationships are vital to us, and we have to care and nurture those relationships - both professionally and personally. In order to help us nurture those relationships, we have to maintain good communication, which can often be misinterpreted to mean that we need to speak when in fact, listening is the most beneficial part of communication. It is often said that there is a reason why we were given two ears and one mouth - we should use them in that ratio.

Think of it this way:

"People do not care how much you know, until they know how much you care."

~ Theodore Roosevelt

We cannot show others that we care unless we have listened to them and have begun to understand who they are.

We do not convert prospects to customers by talking. We need to *listen* to them so that we *understand*, not *listen* just to *reply*. Getting customers is NOT about selling.

Every breakout group also made the comment that '*people buy from people*'. Not everyone likes or gets on with each other, it's all about personalities. If we like someone then we will feel comfortable buying from them. We therefore need to work hard at getting people to like us and a great way to do this is by showing them that you care about them and their needs.

Some other ideas that came out of these groups when it came to converting prospects were:

- <u>Recommendations and Referrals</u> - Once we have built great relationships, trust and respect, we should be asking for recommendations that can be shown to other prospects. We should also ask for referrals. If our customers trust us, then they will feel comfortable recommending us to their friends and business associates.
- <u>Follow ups</u> - We should never think that because we've had one meeting with a potential customer, that's all we need to do. We have to build and nurture these relationships - much like you would an infant - and give them space and time to grow. Great relationships do not happen overnight and it is highly unlikely for us to gain a customer from our first meeting. I once heard it said that follow ups equate to a potential 50% of our business. That's huge.
- <u>Be consistent with your communication</u>, **but be careful what you say** - Remember that your potential customer will have access to everything you put out there, especially on social media, so make sure your messaging is in line with your company and most importantly, is not offensive. Communication on any online platform should be curated without thought of personal financial gain. It's all about building your audience, your platform and your relationships.
- <u>Online Networking/Offline Networking</u> - Such a powerful tool and a great way to make the most of our communication skills. Generally I have found that within networking groups, everyone wants to help each other and are interested in learning as much about their fellow attendees as possible. This leads to collaborative working, offers of help and support plus, the opportunity to be recommended to those in other people's networks.

So, to recap and to help you convert prospects into customers:

» It's all about effective communication and building long term relationships.
» This does not happen overnight. You have to be in it for the long haul.
» Keep a handle on your customer retention and/or conversion percentages. When I sold my business, my retention rate was 90% which was a great metric for understanding how I was performing in the eyes of my clients. Through communication, I learned to look after them.

Having and keeping happy clients is a massive key to success, and it all starts with **listening to understand** rather than **listening to reply**.

~ ~ ~ ~

~ 89 ~

WHY, ONLY WHEN IT REALLY HURTS, DO SO MANY TAKE ACTION?

"I don't count my sit-ups. I only start counting when it starts hurting. When I feel pain, that's when I start counting, because that's when it really counts."
~ Muhammad Ali

I remember someone telling me a story many years ago which really resonated, and I still use it from time to time:

> A guy was walking along the road and he noticed another guy sitting on his porch with his dog. The dog was wailing and moaning. The guy walking past, stopped and spoke to the guy on the porch.
>
> "What's the matter with your dog? Why is it wailing and moaning?"
>
> The guy on the porch replied, "He's lying on a nail."
>
> "Why doesn't he get off?" The first man asked.
>
> "Because it's not hurting enough for him to get off," replied the man on the porch, "it's only hurting enough for him to moan and groan and complain about it."

I'm sure we've all met people like this. They are constantly moaning and groaning - *I'm not making enough money; I don't have enough sales; I can't afford to buy this or that* - but it's obviously not hurting them enough to force them to do something about it. Instead, they just keep moaning.

The question here, then, is what will it take for them to move from the nail?

For some, it is when the things they are moaning about start to directly impact them personally, e.g. when they can't afford to buy food or pay the bills. However, I have come across many who even when things get to that stage will still lie on the nail.

Sometimes, when the nail starts to dig a little deeper, that can be a wake-up call, but there are still far too many who don't move at all - until it is too late. Their business, by this time, will be hanging on by the thinnest of threads and the action of moving away from the nail should have happened months, it not years, sooner.

More often than not, this lack of movement is down to the absence of planning and preparation for which, sadly, they are the only ones to blame.

So, my suggestion to you is to this:

Don't wait for the nail to even start piercing your skin.
Get off the nail well before.

By ignoring this suggestion, I guarantee you will start to feel the nail working its way into your business - probably sooner than you expect. If you want a secure business, one that is 'nail proof', then you need to understand how to build a business properly. To do this, seek out professional help and support from those who know how to run a business.

In my experience, most business owners I have come across have been *technicians*. This means they are skilled at doing what they are good at, but that doesn't necessarily make them a good and responsible business owner.

It's back to the old saying:

Jack of all trades, master of none.

Do what you are good at and stick to just that. By all means learn and get an understanding of the other areas of your business - that is important - but to make things happen, you really need to use other professionals.

When the nail starts to intrude, you might think you can live with the initial sharp pain, however over time, that pain will become stronger and it will begin to spread outwards, encompassing more areas of your business.

So, will you take the time to plan and prepare? Or will you wait until it really hurts?

Only you can answer that question.

~ ~ ~ ~

~ 90 ~

CHANGE ~ ARE OUR BUSINESSES SET UP TO COPE?

"Incredible change happens in your life when you decide to take control of what you do have power over instead of craving control over what you don't."
~ Steve Maraboli

A good friend recently recommended a film called *"The Big Short"* which is based on a true story from the 2008 recession. This got me thinking about how well setup our businesses are to cope with change and situations outside our control.

The most important thing we need to do, is learn from past events. As I've said in many of these articles, we can't continue doing things the way we have always done them as that mentality simply doesn't work anymore.

In the UK alone, there has been an incredible amount of turmoil in the last few years. The business landscape has been altered by significant events such as Brexit and the COVID-19 pandemic - changes that are likely to stay with us whether we like it or not - so we have to find a way to 'go with' them and try not to fight.

Let's look at this in a bit more detail by reflecting on how things have changed in the UK since March 2020 when we first entered lockdown:

*   Personal hygiene became critical to our well-being with high standards remaining in place ever since.
*   Businesses who were reliant on face to face contact with their clients and customers had to find a way around this. Many meetings continue to be conducted online and in some industries, working from home remains the preferred option.
*   Social distancing devastated the hospitality sector, crippling pubs, clubs, hotels, restaurants, events etc.
*   Both personal and business finances were affected. Company's adopted 'furlough' practices in order to help staff survive when they were unable to work.
*   The national debt increased as businesses went under, one by one.
*   Emergency resources were stretched to their limits with many hospitals still recovering from the backlog of cancelled operations and procedures.

The point of note here, is that as businesses, we all learned some hard lessons during the COVID-19 pandemic and we need to use these to our advantage. Though, let me tell you for nothing, that increasing our costs to compensate for reduced revenue will be a very bad move!

It was predicted that we would lose something close to a million small businesses as a result of the pandemic which represents just under a quarter of the total small businesses in the UK. That's a massive hit.

The businesses affected were often those who had continued to do things the way they had always been done and had not moved with the times. This meant there was no flexibility, no disaster plan, no contingencies when the status quo was so brutally challenged. If you are running a business and are uncomfortable making changes, then you could easily end up as a statistic, too.

We all need to change in order to survive and the best way to do this is to seek outside help and support. Be honest about the gaps in your skill set(s) and find reputable outsource options who can plug those gaps. If you don't know who to reach out to, then try attending a local networking event. Not only will you make some great contacts, but you will also be able to ask for recommendations from business owners just like you.

It's about managing the 'what ifs' and pre-empting their arrival so that we can arm ourselves with everything we need to stop them in their tracks.

~ ~ ~ ~

7 Section Seven

Your Business and the Future

91. HOW ARE YOU BUILDING FOR THE FUTURE?
92. HOW WILL YOUR NEXT CHAPTER READ?
93. IT'S TIME FOR A PARADIGM SHIFT
94. SHOULD I QUIT?
95. TOUGH TIMES DON'T LAST, TOUGH PEOPLE DO

~ 91 ~

HOW ARE YOU BUILDING FOR THE FUTURE?

"The future depends on what you do today."
~ Mahatma Gandhi

Ever since the pandemic, I have been asked on several occasions for my advice as to how businesses should recover the money lost during the lockdown period. For me, it's all about your business plan: are you building a short or long term business and do you want to build a client base who trust you?

I've spoken at length about the importance of building business relationships before and it's worth noting here that they are crucial to the future of our businesses. The present of strong relationships will help to shore us up in the tough times but, if we haven't built those relationships, we will very quickly come unstuck.

If you don't have a back up plan for your business and are wondering how you are going to get through the difficult times (because they will come), then here are three pieces of advice I swear by:

1. Read a Personal Development Book

Try to read at least one a month, they are crucial in helping you to prepare for the 'what ifs'. Understanding how others have coped and how you can implement some of these qualities and strategies into your business is a no-brainer. Personal development books really are the building blocks of your business' foundation.

2. Surround Yourself with the Right People

Make sure you surround yourself with people who you can build great relationships with, people who can help and will become part of the growth of your business. Creating your own network is also hugely beneficial if you think you might want to sell your business further down the line.

3. Put Money Away for a Rainy Day

When you start building your business, make sure you put money away for a 'rainy day'. Ideally you should be looking to curate a 6-month slush fund as quickly as possible, with money being deposited into this fund ahead of other 'nice to have' expenditures such as holidays and cars. It won't take long for this fund to be strong enough to support your business and help you rebuild following any damage caused by a major financial event.

Remember:

"The future depends on what you do today."

Make sure you make today and every day count.

Make sure you are prepared for every eventuality – and if you need to, **ask for help.**

~ ~ ~ ~

~ 92 ~

HOW WILL YOUR NEXT CHAPTER READ?

"You can't start the next chapter of your life if you keep re-reading the last one."
~ Michael McMillian

Our lives are like a book - constructed of many chapters - but what many of us don't understand is that we have the power to write the words of our own next chapter. But, the following points are important to remember:

- We need to think very carefully what those words will be.
- We cannot keep living in the past.
- What is done is done.
- The past has no bearing on the future.
- Today is the first day of the rest of our lives.
- Make today and every day count.
- The next chapter requires us to make changes from previous chapters.
- It might require some sacrifices.
- We will not get from where we are to where we want to be with the same mindset that has got us to where we currently are.
- We are in life today exactly where we chose to be because we wrote the words of the previous chapters.
- We are responsible for the decisions we make based on our actions and associations.
- If we don't like where we currently are, then we need to change it.
- We might also need to change some of the people we are associating with.

Competition

Competition doesn't come from other people, it comes from within ourselves. What we also don't realise is that we feed that competition with our actions.

Procrastination - Egos - Unhealthy Food - Knowledge We Neglect - Negative Attitudes - Lack of Creativity - Reluctance to Embrace Change

These are all actions which feed the competition that comes from within ourselves. Most of us do not like change, but '*if we want to change **some** things in our lives, then we need to change **some** things in our lives.*'

<u>Positive Talk = Positive Action = Positive Outcome</u>

What words are coming out of our mouths? What are we saying to other people? What are we saying to ourselves?

We need to be so careful what we are saying – at all times. Positive talk will produce positive action, which will produce positive results. It is from here that we must write our next chapter and we have to remind ourselves that we cannot control external circumstances and events. The only thing we can control is ourselves - the 6 inches between our ears! - which means we have direct control of our thoughts, attitudes and words.

Before we open our mouths, we need to engage our brains and make sure we are using the right words before any wrong words slip through the net. Using the wrong words will not only affect us but the people we are associating with, which may well have a direct impact on the success of our businesses.

When you are writing your next chapter, consider this:

- Get help and support from the right people. Let them be part of the success of that chapter.
- We are not going to get from where we are to where we want to be on our own. We need help and support.
- We need a team of highly professional people on our team. Success is a team effort.
- Let's make sure we pick our team carefully. Find our team through networking.
- Start attending events with a different mindset to those we had before and look at who can add value to our team, to our success.
- We need to stop looking at those we outsource to as a cost, and look at them as an investment in our futures.

If you take these points on board, then there is no reason why you won't write an incredibly successful next chapter - for both your life and your business.

~ ~ ~ ~

IT'S TIME FOR A PARADIGM SHIFT

"Paradigm is a part of the conditioning of the mind,
our conditioning thought patterns."
~ Bob Proctor

I remember reading a book on "Paradigm Shifts" over 20 years ago because I really didn't understand what it was. What I learned was that all great discoveries and paradigm shifts are stimulated by an external event - such as a global pandemic - which almost certainly resulted in many businesses re-thinking how they worked and which created their own paradigm shifts.

Throughout the COVID-19 pandemic it was heart-warming to witness so many businesses create opportunities from such a negative external event. Some employees or small business owners who were furloughed have completely re-evaluated their lives and may now be doing something completely different from what they were doing before the pandemic.

New businesses were also created during this time to meet the paradigm shifts we were making as humans whilst some businesses pivoted to alternative produces or services.

There were those that chose to shut up shop, believing they wouldn't be able to recover from this particular paradigm shift, and there were those who were left with little choice but to cease trading.

Throughout these articles I have covered many ways for business owners to approach unknown changes, and one of the best ways is definitely to create our own paradigm shift. Look at the external event and consider the bigger picture. What can you do or change in your business to meet that external event?

A paradigm shift is all about taking action and taking action is the only way to ensure business longevity and survival. We can, of course, conform and avoid making our own paradigm shifts, but if we do this, we risk being left behind by others who have embraced these changes.

"The Strangest Secret" by *Earl Nightingale* covers this very topic and is a book I highly recommend reading. You can sometimes find this as an audio recording,

too. Either way, you will not be disappointed if you take the time to read or listen to this book. I am certain you will learn something that could really help you to change your mindset and embrace a paradigm shift.

Paradigm shifts can be created by external events which we can react to either negatively or positively.

Alternatively, we can take action before an external paradigm shift arrives by creating our own paradigm shift. If we do this, we will remain in direct control of our lives at all times and, when we do experience another external event, its impact will be significantly lessened because we will have already completed our own paradigm shift.

~ ~ ~ ~

~ 94 ~

SHOULD I QUIT?

"Never, never, never give up."
~ Winston Churchill

The quote for this article comes from a man who was, in my opinion, the greatest leader this country ever had.

Quitting, isn't something that really features in my life. When I decide to do something it's because I really want to do it, so I do it to the best of my ability and I allow it to take as long as it takes.

The same was true of my business. It was something I really wanted to do so I continued running it to the best of my ability until I was ready to sell it on. I've always reminded myself of the following, whether that be for my business or in my personal life:

- Never give up on something you really want to do. Generally, if you give up on something – no matter what you may have said – you obviously did not want it bad enough.
- Never give up on a dream just because of the time it will take to accomplish it. The time will pass anyway. Success is not an overnight thing, and just when you might be on the verge of quitting is the time when a miracle will happen, or the tide will start to turn.

In my experience, the main reason business owners want to quit is because they haven't done enough planning or preparation. It is so true when we say that Prior Planning Prevents Poor Performance and, even though I always made sure to plan for the 'what ifs', there were several occasions when I could have quit.

The first occurred in the early years when I had not been so good at planning. I was also rather naive which resulted in an end of year loss of £24,000 (£75k today). Eek! I wasn't bringing in enough money to cover my overheads so I had a choice: I could quit and go back to working for someone else or I change what I did and the way I did it. The fact I am writing this book tells you that I obviously chose the latter, which meant changing my business offering and my mentality. This was also the point where I started asking for help and surrounding myself with positive, like-minded people who could support my journey.

The second occasion I could easily have quit was a year later when the company who backed my activities went bust to the tune of £2million. The threat to my company was immediate and I once more faced the choice of either working for someone else, or reinventing my business. Again, I chose the latter. This time, though, I was better prepared because I had made those connections and learned those lessons from the first time, which meant I had good people around me who were able to offer sound advice.

There was a third occasion, and this was when the recession hit in 2008/2009. At that time I needed to bring in £50,000 of business a month to cover my £12,000 of monthly overheads, but in April 2009, I brought in only £3,000 worth of business. My accountant told me that if this trajectory continued into the following month, then I would have to shut up shop. Fortunately, due to the preparations and lessons from the previous two occasions, I once more had a contingency plan and was able to tweak a few aspects of my business which enabled me to ride out the recession. It wasn't easy, far from it, but when I came out the other side, I was able to grow the business and leave it as a healthy ongoing concern when I sold it in 2016.

If you feel like you must quit something, then try one of the following:

- Quit making excuses.
- Quit lying to yourself.
- Quit waiting for the right time.
- Quit trying to be perfect.
- Quit trying to fit in.

Just be the person you were born to be.

And never, never, never give up.

~ ~ ~ ~

~ 95 ~

TOUGH TIMES DON'T LAST; TOUGH PEOPLE DO

"Tough times never last, but tough people do."
~ Robert H. Schuller

I am sure we have all been through tough times in our lives, and I am sure we can all testify to getting through them. That doesn't mean we forget those tough times, it's more that we embrace the *'what doesn't kill you makes you stronger'* mentality as we continue on past them.

In terms of business, if you've been running your company for a decent length of time, you'll undoubtedly have been through a number of negative situations, though hopefully these have been cancelled out by a greater number of positives. Even if they haven't yet, they will, because we constantly learn from every (negative) time and can use these lessons to negate and overcome future bumps in the road.

Everything we experience adds to our story, and these are lessons we can pass on to others. I love hearing peoples' stories of how they got started to where they are today, and every one of us has a great story to tell.

Many of these stories will be the result of adversity which gives us the opportunity to reflect on what we have done/achieved since and to be proud of the strength we have gained as a result. Whilst we may not see it at the time, hindsight is a beautiful gift which allows us to understand that without the negative happening, we would never have moved forward. This is when we realise the lesson, and the value of it, that we have learned.

There is a great quote from *Napoleon Hill*:

> *"Every adversity, every failure, every heartache carries with it the seed of an equal or greater benefit."*

From adversity, then, comes growth, but what is it that gets us through those tough times and enables us to realise the resultant growth?

How, for example, did people get through the two World Wars?

What got the Auschwitz survivors through their inhuman experiences?

In my experience, it all boils down to one thing: **a positive attitude.**

If we can hold the belief that things will get better, then we will be able to employ what is our greatest human strength - the power of the mind. The human mind is amazingly resilient and can recover quickly from difficulties, so we have to look beyond where we are and find the proverbial 'light at the end of the tunnel'.

In order to 'look beyond', here's a few tips and tricks:

1. Take care of our mental and physical health.
2. Ask for help if we need to.
3. Limit the time we spend with toxic people or situations.
4. Limit the amount of time we allow our brains to be subjected to negative input. This could mean reducing the time we spend on social media or avoiding the news.
5. Try to eat the right foods for us.

We need to remain tough at all times in order to have a successful business. If we are able to do this **and** add in a healthy body and mind, then we've pretty much cracked it.

If you want to read more on this subject then I highly recommend reading, *"Tough times never last but tough people do,"* by *Robert Schuller.*

Stay strong. Great times are just around the corner.

~ ~ ~ ~

8 Section Eight

Business and Money

96.   COST OR INVESTMENT?

97.   DO YOU KNOW YOUR NUMBERS?

98.   HOW FUTURE PROOF IS YOUR INCOME?

99.   PUT MONEY AWAY FOR A RAINY DAY

100.   TWO SIDES - EVERY DAY IS A SCHOOL DAY - FROM THE HEART

COST OR INVESTMENT?

"Investing in yourself is the best thing you can do. If you've got talents, no one can take them from you."
~ Warren Buffett

How do you look at purchases you make to help you grow your business? Do you view them as a cost or an investment?

Whilst I would always recommend that we invest in ourselves and businesses, I do also think we need to question some of the things we purchase. It can be useful to ask ourselves the question: *are they a worthy spend or have you just bought it/them to impress others?*

I have invested in my education since the age of 23 and have read countless personal development books along the way. For me, the purchase of these books is an investment in me, however, if I had bought the books and never read them, then they would become a cost.

If you take the information you have gleaned from the book and put it into practice, this is a great investment. But, if the book remains firmly wedged in the depths of your bookcase, then you won't have gleaned any information. Thus, your purchase switches from being an investment to being a cost.

Consider your business expenses for a moment - are they are cost or an investment?

As I've mentioned before, the key to running a successful business lies in being able to adapt and evolve and in finding different ways to operate that keep us ahead of the curve. This might mean purchasing some new software, for example. On the face of it, buying the software is a cost and must be subtracted from your bottom line, however, if you are able to use that software to its full advantage and offer different products or services, then it becomes an investment. Think about how much we all needed Zoom during the pandemic. Without Zoom, even more businesses would have struggled to remain afloat, so buying this software (if your needs were greater than the free version) maintained important communication channels which contributed to the survival of so many businesses. The purchase of Zoom, therefore, is arguably a sound business investment.

Engaging trusted suppliers (outsourcing), can also add value to our businesses. Whilst there is an inevitable cost to hire these suppliers, if they are able to complete tasks which will enable us to generate more income, then they are no longer a cost. Outsourcing is an investment, though this can be a difficult concept to square away. If you don't think your business can afford to outsource, consider this:

> Say our business needs a bookkeeper but we are doing the books ourselves because bookkeepers charge between £20 and £30 per hour. Based on the length of time it takes us to complete our monthly books, this is a cost we cannot justify.

> But - whilst a bookkeeper may charge more than we think we can afford, they are a professional and are highly experienced. This means they will finish our books in a much shorter time; maybe two hours to the six it takes you.

> If our chargeable hourly rate is say, £50, then not having to do the books frees up £300 worth of chargeable time (6 x £50). The cost to hire the bookkeeper is £60 (2 x £30), which on paper gives us a net profit of £240. This is how outsourcing becomes an investment rather than a cost.

In order to build a better business *we need to concentrate on what we are good at, what makes us our money* - and outsource everything else. Here are some roles that can be beneficial to outsource:

- A business mentor or coach to keep us on track
- Secure IT support to prevent any unexpected 'crashes' or loss of data
- An HR professional to handle all employment issues
- A social media expert who can deal with all our marketing across multiple platforms

On the flip side, buying a flashy new car to impress your clients is always going to be a cost. Apart from anything else it depreciates in value before it's even been on the road for a day, meaning that when it comes to replacing the car, you're already operating at a net loss. The same is true of unnecessary high-tech equipment. You might think you need it, but chances are it will sit there gathering dust, especially if you don't know how to use it.

And one final tip - don't wait for things to go wrong before you invest in your business (via outsourcing). I guarantee that rescuing your business from a disaster will cost you a heck of a lot more than the investment in professionals, who will help you to build a better business and avoid those disasters.

~ ~ ~ ~

97

DO YOU KNOW YOUR NUMBERS?

"'Know your numbers' is a fundamental precept of business."
~ Bill Gates

I would love to know how many businesses actually know their numbers. I don't just mean the financials, but the numbers relating to areas like sales and orders, too. It constantly amazes me how many businesses bump along from month to month not knowing how much profit they have made or if they have made any at all.

◊ Do you know your conversion rate, for example?
◊ Do you know how many sales you made in a particular month?
◊ Do you know how many clients are in your pipeline?
◊ Do you know the financial size of your market?

I'm guessing some of you reading this will have answered 'NO' to at least one of those questions, yet how can you run a business without knowing these numbers?

The FSB published a statistic a while back which stated that *'88% of all businesses have no idea where they stand financially, at any given moment in time.'*

88%! That means only 12 out of every 100 businesses know the financial state of their business. If we extrapolate this to the number of small businesses in the UK, which is approximately 4.5 million, close to 4 million of these don't have a clue about their numbers.

As *Bill Gates* says, *"'Know your numbers' is a fundamental precept of business"*.

If we don't understand the financials, then we have to employ/outsource to someone who can. This might be a bookkeeper or accountant who can give us all the financial information we need whilst educating us along the way. Knowing our numbers doesn't mean we need to be a qualified accountant, but we should know enough to be able to answer the questions posed above (and other similar ones). Failure to get a handle on our numbers will result in us making really bad financial decisions and spending money we think we have but we don't.

Lack of awareness of our business finances can, at worse, lead to us going out of business and losing our income. This can have a devastating effect not only on us but on our families, too. It could even result in the loss of our relationship, so, for the sake of our businesses and our personal lives, we *have to get a grip* on our numbers.

Here are a few examples of the 'numbers' every good business owner should know:

* Where are our sales coming from?
* How much does it cost to generate a sale?
* Is our marketing working? If so, which aspects?
* What marketing strategy is generating the most leads?
* What is the conversion rate from leads to sales?
* How many new enquiries are we receiving weekly/monthly/annually?
* How long does the on-boarding process take?
* When does each client's revenue mature?

Without knowing these numbers we are constantly batting in the dark. Even if we are aware that more money is coming in than going out so we must be doing okay, imagine how much better than 'okay' our businesses could be doing if we knew these numbers. If we knew what was working and what wasn't, with a bit of greater understanding and tracking, it could mean a day off a week or a longer holiday or time to play golf!

Perhaps you don't necessarily want a 'bigger' business, but how about having a 'better' business? A 'better' business comes from tracking the successes and understanding the failures, so that our business remains viable. This is especially important if we have plans to sell one day.

! **MYTH BUSTER:** *No one expects a business owner to know everything. !*

When it comes to sales, we have to understand who our target market is and we need to promote our business in the places our target market hang out. Having someone on our team who can do this without increasing costs, will be invaluable.

We can only make sensible decisions, though, if we know and understand the numbers. Shouting our message through a megaphone to the wrong people will only cause frustration and achieve nothing. Its important to get this right, and the earlier in our business life we get this right, the better for all concerned.

~ ~ ~ ~

~ 98 ~

·HOW FUTURE PROOF IS YOUR INCOME?

"If you don't find a way to make money while you sleep, you will work until you die."
~ Warren Buffett

The COVID-19 pandemic was a sobering time for us all. The world economies pretty much ground to a halt and over 200,000 people in the UK alone, lost their lives.

This pandemic brought home the importance of our health and well-being and made me, for one, take pause and consider how I would act differently in the future.

If you are a business owner, you have a duty to put processes in place to ensure the health, safety and well-being of every member of staff as well as every visitor or client who enters your premises. If you are an employee, you need to question your employer to make sure they have solid and robust policies in place to protect you. Whilst the majority of responsibility falls to the business owner, it is fair to say that employees have a level of responsibility, too.

Another thing I thought a great deal about during the pandemic was the strength of my revenue stream. You, as a business owner, need to ask yourself if you are doing enough to generate 'good' income, i.e. income that will sustain throughout your life. The pandemic led to millions being furloughed and untold numbers of redundancies, with figures suggesting that upwards of one million businesses have been unable to open their doors since. That's huge.

So, the smart thing to do is to try to protect ourselves from the 'what ifs' and here, from personal experience, is my list of suggestions as to how we do this:

1. <u>LEARN</u> - We must learn from our experiences and make sure we are better prepared for the 'next event'. 'What ifs' will happen and we don't always know when, so making sure we are more prepared than we have ever been is crucial.

2. <u>BE EFFICIENT</u> – We need to run our businesses more efficiently than we have ever done before. Do not try and be all things to all people. We must

focus on doing what we are good at and get professionals in to work on the areas that are not our expertise.

3. SUSTAINABILITY - Look at how your business is structured. Is it sustainable? Is it positioned to be able to handle another "What if?" If it is not, then you need change your business model. Chances are you won't be able to do this on your own, so get expert help. **Remember: if you keep doing what you have always done, you will always achieve the same results. If it's not working, why keep doing it?**

4. ADDITIONAL INCOME STREAMS – Look at other income streams. You need to make sure you have more than one income stream. As the quote says, we need to be able to make money while we are sleeping, so you need to look for an income that will still produce, no matter what. Our main job or business is probably an *active income* so now is the time to look for *passive incomes* as well. There are loads of good opportunities out there.

You need to future proof your income, and the best way to do this is to be better prepared than ever before.

That way, you will have no reason to fear the 'what ifs'.

~ ~ ~ ~

PUT MONEY AWAY FOR A RAINY DAY

"The shortest period of time lies between the minute you put some
money away for a rainy day and the unexpected arrival of rain."
~ Jane Bryant Quinn

Recently I was having a discussion regarding Thorntons, the large chocolate retail chain, which took the decision to close its bricks and mortar stores in 2021 and operate as an online and supermarket supply business only. Inevitably this resulted in a significant number of job losses, however in my experience, the issue with these larger companies is that they have a duty to satisfy their shareholders - which can often lead to their demise.

Small businesses operate slightly differently. Often, they won't have shareholders to pay dividends to, but they will still have expenses and the ever present threat of a recession, or pressures from the changing economy. A lot of small business owners do not plan for the future, and they tend to live for today, which is not necessarily a great way to ensure longevity.

Those of you who of a certain age will remember our parents telling us to, *"put money away for a rainy day"*. Which basically means, saving. If you were anything like me, you probably didn't give it much credence as a child, but isn't it strange how the older we get, the more intelligent our parents become?

I have witnessed first hand, so many businesses who have gone bankrupt because they didn't put any money away for a rainy day. It is my opinion that every business should have a 'rainy day' fund, which should remain untouched until that rainy day. This is a sure fire way to guarantee ongoing business security.

Putting money aside for situations which arise out of the blue is vital for our mental health. Those who don't have a rainy day fund are probably way more stressed than those who have put money aside. The rainy day fund must be topped up before buying the 'nice to have' things, too. That's not to say we can't enjoy the trappings of our success, but we need to remember that our business is like a child - it needs care and nurturing.

When I work with business owners, this is one of the most important messages I impart. Of course, they don't have to take my advice but if they want their business to survive and thrive, they should do.

FACT: Every 8 to 12 years there will be an event that rocks the economy.

If you take into account the pandemic from which the economy is still recovering, then we have a few years (perhaps) to start topping up that rainy day fund.

Putting money away now will make sure you we better prepared when the next rocky period comes along. It is no good waiting for it to happen before we do something about it. The time to act is now.

Business owners should be evaluating their outgoings on a regular basis and looking at ways to cut costs. If you do find a way to save money, then use what you save to add to the rainy day fund.

We should also be considering what our ongoing business strategies are. These need to be in place to ensure generation of new business and income. If you don't know where to start, then talk to others around you who may have some fresh ideas.

Remember: we don't know what we don't know.

A conversation with a colleague or a networking contact costs nothing, but may well provide everything you need to keep that rainy day fund healthy.

~ ~ ~ ~

~ 100 ~

Every day is a school day … especially in business.
But remember: *there are two sides to every story*.

≈◊≈

Here's some final advice to you from me.
Straight from the heart.

As I have stated throughout, these articles were all written during the global Covid-19 pandemic in 2020 and 2021. Many of us found this time incredibly challenging, but it was also an opportunity for reflection and for some businesses, growth.

When the days in lockdown became weeks then months, I allowed myself a moment of pause - a period when I could review my business goals and achievements. At the same time, I considered what it was that I was learning, and how I could use this new knowledge as a 'take away' for my business following those difficult months and years.

The more I thought about it, the more I realised that there were numerous key messages staring me in the face. By extrapolating these, I brought the messages to a point beyond the pandemic and in doing so, created five simple rules. Rules that we can live by both personally and in business.

What I also started to understand was that each of these rules had two sides to them and, in order for us to make the most beneficial decisions, we need to see both sides and then balance our responses accordingly. You'll see what I mean as you work through these rules.

One thing that solidified this to me occurred during the pandemic, when it became apparent that we were only given the information those in power wished for us to have. Rarely were we offered a balanced or alternative view; we simply did as we were told and followed the advice - even when it appeared others were not quite so compliant.

The fallout from the pandemic for businesses - particularly small businesses - was huge and I for one feel that more information should have been readily available. That way, perhaps we would have felt more empowered and in control than we often were. That's not to suggest outcomes would have been different, but at least we would have had those two sides I refer to and would have been able to live or die on our own sword, rather than the ones we were given. As I said, this is just my opinion, but regardless, I think it is important to remember this:

> *There are two sides to every story so, before you do anything, make sure you have all of the facts.*

Here then are my five critical business rules, ratified in part by the pandemic:

Rule One
DON'T BELIEVE EVERYTHING YOU READ OR LISTEN TO

Being a business owner means that you have to think differently, you have to act differently, you need to put your big boy/girl pants on and *sometimes do the very thing that you don't want to do, in order to be successful.*

When you are looking for guidance around important business actions or decisions, it is crucial to remember *not to believe everything you read or listen to.* I honestly believe that a big part of my business and life success is down to me connecting with a personal development programme early on. This gave me the opportunity to work out *who I was, what I wanted* and *how I wanted to achieve it.*

I also got into the habit of reading personal development books over forty years ago, and still do to this day. I listen to positive upbeat motivational material on a regular basis and I try to be careful who I spend my time hanging around with. I came to realise that if I wanted to be successful, I needed to hang around with successful or success minded people BUT CRUCIALLY, I needed to be careful which messages I trusted.

Take the modern-day influencer as a classic example. A quick scroll through any social media platform will convince you that *everyone else is living their best life whilst you are, well, not.* However, if you dig a bit deeper it doesn't take long to realise that much of what is out there is false. It's advertising. A way to sell products. The truth is: *no one has it sorted.*

We absorb millions of messages every day through every sense, so be careful what you read, be careful who you listen to, and be careful what you say. This last one is extremely important because what you say to others, you are also saying to yourself. The poor outcome from negative self-talk is real. Trust me.

Lesson: STAY STRONG TO YOUR BELIEFS

≈ ◊ ≈

Rule Two

BE CONSISTENT

Now, this is really important. If you are not consistent in what you do and how you do it, you will confuse staff, customers and suppliers and no one will know where *you* stand or where *they* stand.

If you don't want to lose respect from the people who really matter in your business you must have a consistent message. When it comes to advertising, its power can only be harnessed if the *right message reaches the right people at the right time*. It is the same with your business message.

» Don't confuse people with a garbled or unclear 60 second elevator pitch at a networking event.

» Don't have an 'idea of the week' or a 'new product of the week' - this is hugely confusing for customers, suppliers, employees ... well, everyone. No one knows where their focus should be.

» Don't keep changing your online or offline marketing message - for exactly the same reason.

However, don't confuse *consistency* with *remaining the same*. It is *important* for your *business to evolve* and for you to *promote different services*, but your *core message* must remain consistent.

Why?

Because no one will understand *what your business is* or *what it does*.

And, if there is a lack of understanding, you risk it becoming an uphill battle to securing clients, regardless of how good your product or service is.

Lesson: MAKE SURE YOUR MESSAGE IS CONSISTENT

≈ ◊ ≈

Rule Three

DON'T FOLLOW THE MASSES TO BE PART OF THE CROWD

Being a business owner and breaking out from the masses takes courage. Most of us sit in this bubble of mediocrity and when we try and break out of it, there are a number of people grabbing hold of us, trying to pull us back in.

Why? Because there is safety in numbers. Whilst our friends want to see us achieving and becoming successful, they do not want to see us becoming more successful than them.

Think about that for a moment and then consider a time when you made a brave decision or ventured into the unknown. For every one person cheering you on and telling you that you could do it, I bet there were many more telling you to be careful and not to risk everything.

It takes courage to be a small business owner, particularly because many of us are great 'technicians' in what we do, but that doesn't necessarily make us great business owners. Once you take that leap and strike out on your own, it is *true that you are unlikely to regret it BUT*, you will find yourself in a position where you suddenly need to know everything about everything. Which simply isn't possible. This is why I am always advising the small business community to stop trying to be all things to all people - a theme which you will have seen often in the previous 100 articles.

The bottom line is this: *get help for the stuff you are not good at*.

If you don't, there is every chance that you will regret the decision to go your own way. You will struggle mentally, physically and financially and will undoubtedly wish that you'd listened to the naysayers (or remained part of the crowd).

However, it doesn't need to be that way. You made your decision to stand out for a reason so please, if you can, keep going, get help and speak to someone you trust.

If you keep believing in yourself, keep working (through those tough times), keep looking for opportunities and keep building relationships, you will never regret moving away from the crowd.

Lesson: ENSURE YOU STAY COURAGEOUS

≈◊≈

Rule Four

RELATIONSHIPS - WHY THEY ARE SO IMPORTANT

It is both my opinion and experience, that strong trusting relationships are everything. Some would disagree; there are many sales techniques and tactics which achieve results without spending time building relationships, however, that is not how I chose to run my business. I remain convinced that developing relationships is the key to a successful business and most importantly, to its longevity.

If you've been in business for any length of time, someone will undoubtedly have reminded you that *'people do business with people'* who they *'know, like and trust'*, and I cannot endorse these sentiments enough. No matter how much technology changes the business landscape, I firmly believe that first and foremost we will always continue to work with those we *'know, like and trust'*.

For me, there is now far too much reliance on technology - no one seems to use common sense or make decisions anymore - yet I don't see how this practice can be anything other than short-sighted and counter-productive.

When I was actively selling for my advertising business, I always preferred to walk away from a sale and maintain a relationship with a client if I didn't believe in that sale. In other words, if I felt that whatever I was promoting to a client would not work for them or give them value for money, I would walk away.

Granted, that is not always easy to do, particularly if you are struggling when it comes to your bottom line, but here's a great piece of advice I was given in the early days:

'To put myself in every client's shoes' and to take my eyes off myself.'

In simple terms, if I knew I wouldn't like the proposed outcome on the other side of the deal (i.e. if I were the customer), then I needed to either change my proposition (for the customer) or walk away. I continued to apply this advice throughout my forty plus years as a business owner and I know that it put me in good stead. Not only that, I was able to conduct myself and my business in a way I felt comfortable with and proud of.

When you stop thinking about yourself, you will begin to notice a by-product: *others will be more willing to help and support you when you need it and ultimately smooth your path to getting what you want.*

Give, in order to get.

I have never sold anything with the sole aim of lining my own pocket, and I would strongly advise against doing business with anyone who operates this way. If they are only out for themselves, you can't ever be sure they are trustworthy.

Lesson: WE WORK WITH PEOPLE THAT WE KNOW, LIKE & TRUST

≈ ◊ ≈

Rule Five

BE BRAVE ENOUGH TO CHANGE YOUR MIND

Sometimes, we need to be brave enough to change our minds. If what we are doing is not working or we are not getting the response we are expecting, we have to change it in some way.

If you find yourself stuck and wanting to change but don't know how, try looking at business trends around you. Notice what your competition is doing. Is this benefiting them? Is it having a positive or negative impact?

Another way to move forward is to take a moment to *really hear* what your clients are saying. Listen to what they *need* and *what they are asking for* and then consider what it would take to *deliver* that. Then, when you deliver, do it in such a way that makes you stand out from the crowd.

However, exercise caution when it comes to simply following trends that are working. You need to consider if these trends are 'past their best' or have 'had their day' because the last thing you want to do is play catch-up on a trend that is about to be superseded by another.

The way to get ahead, to be the trendsetter if you like, is to maximise your potential by doing something different. Think outside of the box and do your market research. Take some time to brainstorm ideas so that when it comes to making those changes, you will be setting a path for others to follow, rather than being the one who is playing catch-up.

Re-visit the pandemic years, for example, and look up stories of companies who pivoted their businesses. Whilst this was (often) necessary for survival, some achieved better results than others because they did things that little bit differently. If there's one thing I can guarantee, it's that those businesses which stand still and don't change their minds are always going to be ill-equipped to deal with inevitable uncontrollable events such as recessions and pandemics. Therefore, it is critical to your business' survival to change your mind. Those who did so during the pandemic are the ones who remain in business today.

Remember:

- *Changing your mind is not a sign of weakness, nor is it an indicator of failure.*

- *Success never runs in a straight line, nor should your business.*

- *Be prepared. Watch out for forks in the road and don't be afraid to take a 90 or even 180 degree corner.*

Lesson: IF YOU CAN'T CHANGE YOUR MIND, THEN YOU ARE NOT USING IT

≈ ◊ ≈

Closing Thought:

No matter what you go through for the rest of your lives, stay strong to your beliefs and spend time with real people who 'lift you up' rather than social media-type friends who will almost certainly drag you down.

From The Heart. From Me To You. **Be You**. **Do You**.

www.ingramcontent.com/pod-product-compliance
Lightning Source LLC
Chambersburg PA
CBHW040850210326
41597CB00029B/4794